How I Pioneered America's Craft Brewing Industry, Opened the First Brewpub, Bucked Trends, and Enjoyed Every Minute of It

THE ALE MASTER

With
ROBERT SPECTOR

THE ALE MASTER

How I Pioneered America's Craft Brewing Industry, Opened the First Brewpub, Bucked Trends, and Enjoyed Every Minute of It.

Printed in the United States
Distributed in Canada by Raincoast Books Ltd.

Author: Bert Grant with Robert Spector
Foreword: Michael Jackson
Editor: Judy Gouldthorpe
Cover design: Karen Schober
Interior design: Paul Langland
Technical editor: Benjamin Myers
Publisher: Barry Provorse
Produced by: Documentary Book Publishers

Library of Congress Cataloging-in-Publication Data
LC# 98-30353
Grant, Bert, 1928-
The ale master: how I pioneered America's craft brewing industry, opened the first brewpub, bucked trends, and enjoyed every minute of it/Bert Grant, with Robert Spector.

ISBN 0-935503-23-4

1. Grant, Bert, 1928- 2. Brewers—United States—Biography.
I. Spector, Robert, 1947- . II. Title.

Sasquatch Books
615 Second Avenue
Seattle, Washington 98104
(206) 467-4300
e-mail: books@SasquatchBooks.com
www.SasquatchBooks.com

Sasquatch Books publishes high-quality cookbooks, exceptional travel books, nonfiction and children's books related to the Pacific Northwest. For more information about our titles and services, contact us at the address listed above, or view our site on the World Wide Web.

THE ALE MASTER

CONTENTS

FOREWORD

As a newspaperman, I was at first just an amateur beer-drinker. It was only gradually that I turned professional. More than 20 years, about 10 books, a similar number of documentary films and about a thousand articles later, I struggle to remember everything I have learned about beer.

"How did you study?" people ask me. "By drinking a lot, a different beer every day, and sometimes rather more," I answer, only half-joking. "And by the good journalistic practice of poking my nose into other people's work and asking them questions." I was unknown to the first brewers I badgered. Some dismissed me, and others were helpful and open far beyond self-interest. One of the first brewers to be really helpful was a Scot. "When you are not making beer, what is your hobby?" I asked. "At home, I make wine," he replied. That was not Bert Grant, but the same enthusiasm and eclecticism applies. The greatest brewers I have met are people with passions as insistent as a laser, individuals harder to cut into shape than a diamond. In my experience.

Bert is one of the all-time greats. That is why he has made such great beer, in such distinct styles, been such a pioneer in the brewpub movement, and been one of the most powerful inspirations in the American Beer Revolution of the 1980s and 1990s.

Being myself a keen practitioner of stubbornness, I admire that perhaps more than any other characteristic. Bert is immovable, opinionated, provocative, fearless and utterly sure of his ground. In a world of focus groups, dumbing-down and marketing-speak, Bert is a beacon of human cussedness. I spend time with him at every opportunity. We have wandered the pubs of London, sampled secret brews in New York hotel rooms, and ridden over the Cascade Mountains in a Rolls-Royce with a license plate saying REAL ALE.

"Sample this beer! Nose those hops!! Bite that apple!!! Drink that wine!!!!" Yes, Bert, but could I just take a break and read your book? I want to remember what I have learned from you.

—Michael Jackson

London, England, 1998

For more than 50 years, I've been working to share the pleasure I get from a pint of distinctive beer. I hope you enjoy drinking Bert Grant's Ales as much as I enjoy brewing them.

INTRODUCTION

I became a "microbrewer" before the public knew what the term meant. Back in 1982, a few partners and I installed a small-batch brewery in an old opera house in Yakima, Washington, a town better known as the hop-growing capital of the USA. How small? We could brew about eight kegs at a time. The beers from that humble beginning carry my name, Bert Grant.

A lot of people will tell you that our little ramshackle brewery—our neighbors included a pool hall and a bordello!—was revolutionary. Depending on whom you ask, it was either the first, second or third microbrewery to open in North America. But it definitely was the first "brewpub" to open in the United States since the repeal of Prohibition.

Today, brewpubs are found in every major American city. And chances are good that, when you look at any supermarket beer cooler or pop into your favorite bar or restaurant, you'll find at least a microbrew or two: hand-crafted ales and lagers, bocks, Pilsners, porters, stouts, ambers and more—some even made by the country's largest breweries. Consumers can choose from a selection of fresh-brewed beers (including my own Bert Grant's Ales) in a dizzying array of styles, colors, flavors. No doubt, the micros, or "craft beers," are here to stay.

I've been called a lot of things over the years since we first fired up our five-barrel copper brewkettle: maverick, beer pioneer, "colorful," "stubborn" (and some other terms I won't reprint here). *The Wall Street Journal* even named me "a patriarch of the micro movement." But I prefer the recognition from my peers as "Dean of America's Craft Brewers."

What are the secrets of my success? Unique ingredients, special techniques, patented hop varieties? Not really. There's nothing particularly arcane about the brewing process. In my case, it all boils down to one thing: I brew all my ales to please the most demanding palate I have ever encountered in over 50 years in this business—my own. To my taste, my beers are the best. Even if you disagree, you must admit that they are distinctive.

Too many beers, especially at the world's largest breweries, are designed to appeal to the broadest number of people. They've been stripped of the idiosyncrasies and distinctive characteristics that make beer such an interesting and enjoyable drink. I'll never forget a meeting I attended years ago with the top executives of one of North America's biggest brewers, when the senior vice president of marketing put it as plainly as you could get: "*I want a beer that nobody can object to*."

I take the opposite approach. Beer should reflect the taste of the brewer. Consequently, I don't brew wimpy beers. Each one has a unique taste and character, designed to be savored slowly. (In fact, there is a story behind every Bert Grant's Ale, as you'll discover in this book.) You may not enjoy all my beers, but when you find one you like, I expect you will be pleased.

At its best, brewing is a balance of science and art. The scientist needs a combination of the best ingredients, the best equipment and the best know-how. The artist needs the passion and the instinct to create. Beer is almost a living thing. It does change, even in the bottle. Compare that to something like Coca-Cola, with a formulation that is almost bullet proof. There're no nutrients in there to allow fermentation. The pH is low enough so that nothing else is going to grow in it. You can put it on a warm shelf or in the sun, and the flavor won't change. I'll wager that if you put a can of Coca-Cola in a bomb shelter, it would still be drinkable in 50 years. Most people I know wouldn't want a beer like that.

All of our ales are hand-crafted in a single 40-barrel, direct-fire copper kettle (which provides the most even heat) from my own recipes. I don't feel it is possible to make much more than 150 barrels in a single batch and still do a good job. I prefer batches of 40 to 50 barrels. The Germans and Japanese have created computer systems so that thousand-barrel batches can all be done by automation; all that many of today's brewmasters have to do is punch a button marked "porter" or "hefeweizen" and off it goes . . .

I like to produce on a smaller scale so that everything is controlled by the brewer, not by the computer people, the accountants or the MBAs. These people should be *drinking* the brewer's beer, not making it.

GLOSSARY

Beer: *Any fermented beverage made from grain, almost always seasoned with hops. Beer is divided into two basic categories: ales, which are "top-fermented," and lagers, which are "bottom-fermented."*

Ale: *Any beer fermented at relatively warm temperatures (approximately 60-75 degrees F; 15-24 degrees C), which promote yeast activity, create rapid fermentations, and produce aromatic and/or flavor compounds (esters) in addition to carbon dioxide and alcohol.*

Wort: *Pronounced "wert." The sugar-rich liquid created by steeping grain (barley malt, etc.) in hot water, usually in a vessel called a mash tun or mash cooker. ("Mash" is the mixture of grain and water.) The wort usually is separated from the "spent" grain in a second vessel called a lauter tun.*

Brewkettle: *The vessel wherein the wort is boiled with the hops. This usually takes around one and a half hours. Boiling breaks down certain hop compounds and allows them to be absorbed into the wort.*

Brewpub: *A pub or restaurant offering food alongside beers brewed and served on the premises.*

Fermenter: *A specialized tank used for the fermentation process, usually with variable temperature control.*

Yeast: *A single-celled organism that "eats" the sugar in the wort, and produces carbon dioxide and alcohol as by-products (along with other aroma and flavor compounds).*

Hops: *Generally refers to the cones of the mature hop vine, which are used to "season" beer and provide bitterness to balance the malty-sweetness of the wort.*

My goal always has been simple: I want to make the best beer I can with the best ingredients I can find, regardless of cost. When it comes to hops, I push my beers to their limits—beyond their limits, some people say—to bring out their distinctive characteristics. It's possible to overhop a beer, I guess, but it would take an awful lot of hops to do it.

Overall, I'm optimistic. I believe the tastes of North American beer drinkers are becoming more sophisticated. During the past decade, we've seen an explosion of small breweries making full-flavored beers to meet new demand. Of course, there are still plenty of people who have yet to learn to enjoy what craft beers offer—just as there still are people who drink instant coffee instead of freshly ground Starbucks. I'm reminded of this gap when I'm sitting in my brewpub in Yakima, Washington, and someone says, "Bert, I don't like your Imperial Stout." I answer with a smile: "That's okay. Someday your taste buds will grow up." It's a natural progression; it shows that the market has room to mature. Just look at the Europeans, with their thirst for great beers and all the small breweries working to quench it.

How did I get to be such a know-it-all on the subject of brewing? Why did Portland's newspaper *The Oregonian* dub me "the godfather of the Northwest beer boom"? The answers are in this book. Since you're reading these words, you're obviously interested in beer. So, come on along for a trip through the past half-century of this business, through the rise, fall and rise of the craft-brewing industry.

MICHAEL JACKSON ON BERT

Bert was the first of the new-generation North American craft brewers to be a really knowledgeable, experienced brewer. A lot of the best people in this upstart industry had no brewing background at all, just a desire to make good beer. Some of the worst have been either people with very good marketing backgrounds or, in some instances, people with very good brewing backgrounds. An awful lot of people from the mainstream brewing industry got into it, and had no idea how to hack this scale of operation, and thought they knew everything.

The difference with Bert is that he's such a maverick. He brings the combination of individualism and perfectionism and love of beer on the one hand, and technical brewing experience on the other hand, particularly about hops. He has developed a range of brews in classic styles, each with his own stubbornly idiosyncratic twist. He brews beer only for his own taste. If there is a single key to success in microbrewing, that's probably it.

In Belgian mythology there is a creature called a Hop Devil, which is actually a personification of the creature who threatens the hops. But over the years, it's become an almost beloved figure. With his slightly demonic quality, Bert is a kind of Hop Devil.

Michael Jackson is the host of the television program *The Beer Hunter*, and an award-winning author of books on beer, whiskey and travel, including *Michael Jackson's Beer Companion* and *The Simon & Schuster Pocket Guide to Beer*. He is the first winner of the achievement award from the Institute for Brewing Studies.

My family in Toronto, Canada, 1939 (l to r): My mother Lizzie, me (11 years!), brother Jimmy (8), and father Lewis.

Chapter One

A CHEMICAL REACTION

I was born in Dundee, Scotland, in 1928 to Lewis and Elizabeth (Lizzie) Grant. When I was an unhappy, colicky baby, Mother used to give me a small amount of single-malt Scotch mixed with honey, which instantly transformed my disposition. (It still does.) So, I got started very early on the "single-malt remedy," which was common back in those days. Today, they'd probably arrest a mother for giving her child a sip of whiskey.

Mother's family were dairy farmers. They delivered their milk in big tanks to customers who filled up their own bottles. Most of her family eventually emigrated to Australia.

My father's family were highlanders, who worked in mills that made jute fiber backings for rugs and carpets. The raw material, the hemp, was bought in India and Pakistan, and woven (not smoked!) in the big mills in Scotland—Dundee in particular. Eventually, the mills' British owners decided it was cheaper to weave the jute in India than it was in Scotland, and the industry in Dundee disappeared.

Before I reached the age of two, we moved to Toronto, following my dad's older brother, Jimmy, who had already settled there. I grew up on Dermott Place, where just about everybody on my street was an immigrant, from Scotland, Ireland or Italy. I became a real city boy, and was soon able to get anywhere in town by streetcar, bicycle or foot.

My love affair with beer began at a precocious age. My dad let me drink any beer in our house that was left in open bottles by him or his friends. One New Year's Day, when I was about six or seven years old, he caught me opening a bottle. Boy, did he get mad! He laid down the rule: I was forbidden from opening any bottles. If the bottles were *already* open, then it was okay.

My mother worked in a tiny fish-and-chips shop, while my father worked a series of odd jobs. He was always going from one job to another, doing whatever he could to make a living. Although he never made much money, he taught me the value of honest hard work, and he was quite proud of the fact that he never received unemployment benefits from the government, which was commonly referred to as "the dole." In fact, the one thing that he told me that I've always remembered was, "If you ever go on the dole, I'll come and beat you!" Now that I think about it, that admonition was pretty good motivation for becoming an entrepreneur.

QUALITY OF LIFE

I don't drink cheap whiskey. I learned that from my old man. We may have been poor, but he would never have cheap whiskey in the house. He always said, "Either it will be good Scotch or none." I think that's a great attitude to have.

PATIENCE

Patience—the quality that every brewmaster needs—I learned from my mother. She taught me all about cooking, which became an important part of my early life. From the time I was a small child, I watched—and learned—as my mother prepared simple, but delicious, dishes from the old country.

One of my favorites was lentil soup, which was loaded with carrots, potatoes, lentils and, most important, a ham bone. Neither my mother nor I liked a lot of fat, so she took the time to cool the mix and skim the fat off the broth. Mother cooked that ham bone for a week before adding the lentils, and that mix boiled at least a day before the vegetables were added. The soup pot sat on the back of the stove, simmering away for days and days and days before it hit its peak. If I close my eyes, I can still smell the wonderful aromas of my mother's kitchen.

It was marvelous soup, but it wouldn't have been nearly as good without one essential ingredient: *patience*. And that's just what you need to brew great beer.

Science

When I was growing up, I was fascinated with chemistry and biology. I knew early on that I was going to be a scientist. One of my proudest days was when I was 10 years old and got my *adult* library card, which meant I was no longer restricted to the children's shelves. So, I devoured all the science books—chemistry, physics, biology—and any reference books that I could take home with me. By grade seven, I was doing fairly sophisticated chemistry.

I lived down the street from the local Owl Drug Store. Back in those days, pharmacists were called "chemists," and they were always well stocked with chemicals of all sorts. On my way home from school, I would go behind the drugstore, scavenge through the garbage cans, and retrieve any chemicals that had been thrown out. Everything was labeled. Over the years, I was able to put together a beautiful chemistry set. Using chlorates and nitrates, I created my own explosives and firecrackers to celebrate Dominion Day and the Queen's birthday. By the time I got into high school, I was combining nitric acids and sulfuric acids and glycerin to produce the kind of "homegrown" explosives favored by political radicals—all in the name of scientific experimentation, of course.

My natural inclination to chemistry found an ideal outlet in the challenging Central Technical School, which was chock-full of excellent students. In those days, you had to pass each class every year to advance. If you failed, you had to leave school. There was no such thing as keeping you back or repeating a year!

From grades 10 through 12, I had a very clever chemistry teacher named Dr. Self, who was one of my early mentors. Whatever question you had, he would answer it with patience and precision. Dr. Self gave me my first opportunity to do industrial research. When I was 13, a couple of classmates and I were given the assignment of analyzing silica in aeronautical aluminum for the airplane industry. It was a tricky method that involved boiling hydrochloric acid, and they didn't give that job to amateurs.

What I like about chemistry is the logic of it. Chemicals are not random. If you know the periodic table, you can pretty well predict how two elements are going to react when you put them together. If you combine two elements from opposite ends of the table, they are going to go "bang." It's very logical.

To a degree, my appreciation for the logic of chemistry carries over to the logic of beer. If you stick to a brewing formula, you are pretty much going to duplicate what's called for. The art of brewing comes when you add your personal touch and preference to modify the formula, and you know what will result. That's what's so satisfying to me about the brewing process.

A portrait of the brewer as a young man!
In my "senior lab technician" days
at Canadian Breweries, Toronto, 1950.

Chapter Two

YOU GET PAID TO DO WHAT?

In November of 1944, as the Second World War was raging, the head of the chemistry department at Central Technical School came into our chemistry class and asked me to step outside. There, I met a fellow who was the right-hand man of Mr. E. P. Taylor, the chairman of Canadian Breweries, the biggest brewing company in Ontario. The gentleman had asked to speak with the school's best chemistry student. That would be me, of course. I was already doing second-year university chemistry.

He told me that because so many able-bodied men had gone to fight in the war, the chemistry department of Canadian Breweries' Carling division—which was considered one of the best in the world—was short-handed. Right there on the spot, he offered me a job in the chemical analytical area, where I would modify methods to make them easier and more accurate, and analyze beer for sugar, alcohol and yeast content.

If I took the job, I would be graduating from school in January instead of June. Since I already had enough credits to graduate, it made sense to start my working career because I knew that I couldn't afford to go to college.

Canadian Beer Industry

After the repeal of Prohibition, Edwin Plunkett (E. P.) Taylor inherited the ownership of Brading's Brewery from his uncle. He formed the Brewing Corporation of Canada, and set out to dominate the national market by "eliminating the competition." That year, he acquired seven breweries (including Carling) in Ontario, and two in Manitoba, closing some of the small, inefficient plants but maintaining all the labels. He was essentially buying brands and production facilities, consolidating and building bigger, more efficient breweries. He later did the same thing in Quebec. He eventually changed the name of the company to Canadian Breweries Limited, which acquired O'Keefe Brewing and National Breweries Limited, whose best-known brand names were Dow and Dawes of Quebec.

According to Stephen Beaumont's Great Canadian Beer Guide, *by the early 1950s, Taylor, who reorganized all of his Quebec operations under the name Dow Brewing Company, swallowed about 30 rivals and reduced the number of available brands from 150 to 8.*

At about the same time, I was offered a prestigious job as an apprentice gold assayer because I was the top student in my assaying class. The assaying job was tempting because it was for more money than the $90 a month for a five-day week that Canadian Breweries offered me. But I would have had to move to far northern Ontario, where there was 2 months of summer and 12 months of isolation. Preferring to stay in the city, I chose beer over gold, and I've never regretted it. After all, you can't drink gold.

On the other hand, I could drink all the beer I wanted. Each morning, as part of our sensory-analysis program, I tasted 50 to 100 beers—a job that was not bad on the whole, but a bit tiring. Because I was only 16—and the drinking age was 21—I could *make* beer and I could even take it home, but I couldn't *buy* it. When I went back to high school and told everybody about my job, they couldn't believe it. "You get paid to do *what*?" To them, it was the dream job: tasting beer and getting paid for it.

Good Beer, Bad Beer

Of course, the reality was much more sobering. I became an authority on *bad*-tasting beer. By spending a good portion of my day looking through a microscope and examining bacteria-infected fermented samples, I learned how to recognize the smell and taste of bad beer, and how to correlate that information with what I saw under the microscope, and how to keep distinctive yeast strains pure.

To this day, I don't hesitate to criticize other people's beer if it has problems. I always try to be diplomatic, but I also always try to tell the truth. (Sometimes those goals are mutually exclusive.) When somebody from a microbrewery or a home brewery brings me a foul-smelling beer, I don't even have to taste it to know it's "off" because I've been through these situations too many times. From time to time, when I was quality-control manager for Carling Brewing, I would have to go into one of our plants and tell the brewmaster that he was producing bad beer, inform him about what was causing the problem, and explain what should be done to correct it. They didn't always agree with me, but I was usually right.

I knew immediately after I started that I wanted to spend the rest of my life in the brewing business. I liked everything about my job because it was a constant, endless challenge. Canadian Breweries bought their hops primarily from the U.S. (California and the Yakima Valley) and British Columbia, as well as small amounts from England and Czechoslovakia. At most of our plants, we used a blend of at least eight different varieties of hops in each brew. I love the fact that you can study hop chemistry all your life and still not know everything. There is so much to learn.

WHAT ARE HOPS?

When Ancient Greek and Roman historians wrote of blossoming garden plants that emitted an ethereal, spicy aroma, they were undoubtedly referring to hops. Historically, all sorts of herbs and spices have been added to beer either to produce special flavors or to cover up "off flavors" caused by bacteria or undesirable yeasts.

Hops rose to prominence as the main "spice" for beer as brewers empirically discovered that hopped beers showed improved foam stability, better clarity, and improved storability and stability. (We now understand the chemistry of certain hop compounds that cause these results.)

Hops have been cultivated in America since the arrival of the first European settlers, who brought along their homeland's brewing techniques. Hop farming moved westward with the country's expansion. Thanks to its beneficial growing conditions (coupled with a readily available source of local labor, important before the introduction of mechanized picking), the Pacific Northwest today is America's "hop pocket." Close to 75 percent of the U.S. hop crop grows in Washington's Yakima Valley (with smaller percentages in Idaho and Oregon).

Each year, hop farmers build an intricate array of 18-foot-high wire trellises, which are eventually covered by hop vines. Under good conditions, the hop vines grow so rapidly (up to a foot per day) that you can literally watch it happen. They start to sprout from their roots in April, run up the wires by the end of May, and ripen in the last part of August. Then the vines are cut down, and their cones, or "blossoms," are harvested, dried and baled for future use. The cones, which look like a cross between a flower and a little green pine cone, contain oils that provide flavor and aroma to beer, and certain natural compounds that provide bitterness.

One of the strange things about hops is that there is nothing in hop oil that can't be found in cinnamon oil, clove oil or any of the other essential oils. About 90 percent of the compounds in hop oil exist in something else. The proportions are all different. In clove oil and cinnamon oil there is about a 90 percent overlap between compounds. There, it's the quantitative difference that accounts for the difference in flavors. But the hop's lupulin glands are distinctive. The lupulin contains bittering compounds (humolones and lupulones) that are not found in anything else. Chemists and brewers have been looking for humolones in something other than hops for a hundred years, preferably in something that's cheaper to grow, but it can't be found.

I later did extensive studies in microbiology and became fascinated with bacteria and yeast. I eventually became assistant director of microbiological quality control for Canadian Breweries.

The Triumph of the Bean Counters!

As North American beers became lighter and less full-bodied, I was getting fed up with the mass brewing industry, which was no longer being run by the brewers but by the accountants—who wanted brewers to produce larger batches with fewer and less expensive ingredients.

For example, when I started in this business, there was no mucking about with the brands. Carling brewed a copper-colored ale called Dominion White Label, which was, by our analysis, the most heavily hopped beer in Toronto (with English Fuggles, Kent Goldings and other hop varieties). But then the bean counters began running the company in overzealous pursuit of "efficiencies" and profits. When word came down that they were going to drop Dominion White Label, it signaled the triumph of the mass-production mind-set, which meant cutting corners and costs and eliminating its sense of tradition. Not surprisingly, sales of reformulated White Label slumped sharply; it was a self-fulfilling prophecy.

The same thing happened to most of the big brewers. The best-tasting beer was watered down for the masses, and brewing was becoming a "push-button" business, with automated breweries and liquid hops concentrate. But that's a story for later.

Hold the Corn Syrup!

By the 1960s, the big brewers were popularizing the use of flavor-diluting additives such as rice flour and corn syrup. When I was working for Canadian Breweries in the late 1950s, we did some pilot brewing with refined corn syrups and discovered that they contributed absolutely nothing to the taste of the beer. So, if you ran a brew with 70 percent malt and 30 percent corn syrup and another with a 50:50 ratio, all you did was dilute the flavor of the malt—like diluting a 100 percent malt beer with carbonated water. The only thing that corn contributed—because of its fermentable material—was pure alcohol. So brewers found that they could use corn, cut down the amount of barley malt, and get the same amount of alcohol in the finished beer at a lower cost. The only thing you're sacrificing is flavor.

By the mid-1950s, I was becoming disillusioned with the company, thanks to all the bean-counting. Around the same time, the Canadian government decided that E. P. Taylor was too big. So, instead of making him break up Canadian Breweries, the government ruled that the three divisions—Carling, O'Keefe's and Brading's—had to have separate marketing, sales, purchasing and production staff. The result was that the three companies started cutting each other's throats, competing amongst themselves as bitterly as they battled Labatt's and Molson's, the other two dominant Canadian brewing companies. That internecine warfare ultimately was a big factor in the demise of the company. For me, all these circumstances, along with the dumbing-down of our beers, meant that it was time to move on.

THE GREAT CONTINUOUS BREWING EXPERIMENT

George Stein, who has known Bert since the mid-1950s, was a long-time salesman of centrifuges, which in the brewing industry are used on a large scale to remove yeast and other sediments from liquid during the beer-making process. George, who later became his business partner, recalls Bert's trials and tribulations in selling his theories on continuous brewing to his bosses at Canadian Breweries:

In the late 1950s, everyone was experimenting with continuous brewing concepts. Canadian Breweries, using Bert's pilot brewery, was on the leading edge. By 1958, Bert's 12-gallon-a-day fermentation system had been proven to make excellent-quality beer for several months at a time. We then convinced the production department to increase the continuous brewing output. We were given the use of a cellar that had four open ale tanks, each with a capacity of about 400 barrels. With some simple modifications, two of these tanks could produce more beer than six or seven could ordinarily produce.

Although we ultimately didn't have a great deal of success, we had a great time. When they were testing the continuous brewing process, somebody had to be in the brewery 24 hours a day. But Bert's system was so simple to run, and so foolproof, that the brewers didn't have much to do. The evening and night shifts often turned into all-night parties!

Everything came to a head in 1959, when I was helping Canadian Breweries experiment on advanced brewing methods, including continuous fermentation. With the help of my friend George Stein, who sold centrifuges, I devised a lovely system of making the beer continuously. After successfully running the continuous brewing operation in the pilot brewery, we got permission to put the operation in Canadian Breweries' O'Keefe brewing plant, where it worked beautifully for several months. Although the beer produced by continuous brewing showed slight differences from that of traditional production, the powers-that-be at Canadian Breweries judged—through a series of tastings—the beer to be clean in flavor and of excellent quality.

Eventually, the powers-that-be had a meeting to decide the fate of continuous brewing. After we tasted the beer, they politely asked me to leave the room, which I did (exiting with the comments of "Great beer, Bert" ringing in my ears). I returned to the lab.

In the meantime—unbeknownst to me—the Canadian Breweries executives brought in a self-proclaimed brewery "expert" from New Zealand who claimed to have developed his own continuous brewing process. The executives decided at that meeting that they would tear out all of my equipment and replace it with equipment specified by the New Zealander. When I found out, I did the only self-respecting thing—I quit!

(By the way, the New Zealander's system was installed and tried for a year. The results were so poor that the whole thing eventually was scrapped. I later found out that the company paid millions of dollars for a method that was not even patented.)

One of the joys of my time at Canadian Breweries was designing, building and running the company's experimental breweries. The day I left, they shut down the continuous brewing brewhouse in Montreal because nobody else wanted to be responsible for running it. But my work with experimental breweries lived on. It helped me try countless brewing ideas that would become the foundation of the ales that would eventually bear my name.

"EXTRACTLY" RIGHT!

Canada has always had an odd attitude about beer. Unlike the U.S., which has pubs and taverns for food, drink and entertainment, Canada, for many years, just had beer halls. These were watering holes—for men only—that didn't serve food and didn't provide entertainment, not even darts. You just sat at a table and drank beer. The idea was to create an atmosphere where people wouldn't drink too much beer. Writing in The Great Canadian Beer Book, *Harry Bruce described these beer halls as "sad, sour, lethargic joints" that were usually found "underground, where worms, moths and centipedes lived."*

The beer wasn't always that great, either. George Stein, one of my old friends in the beer business, once frequented a Toronto beer hall that served a light ale with very little hops. He complained to me about that beer, and I told him I could fix it. I had taken to carrying around my own liquid hop extract formulation in a little eye dropper bottle and putting a drop in somebody else's brew—just to improve it, of course.

So, I sent a vial of the extract to George, who went into the beer hall the next day and said to the waiter, "Before you pour that, let me put a drop in the glass," which he did. The waiter poured the beer into the glass, and the extract dissolved quickly.

"He asked what I was doing," recalled George. "Then I told him to taste that beer and compare it to one of his. He couldn't believe the difference."

While running Stroh's pilot brewery in the early 1960s, I experimented with many forerunners of today's famous Yakima Valley hop varieties.

Chapter Three

EXPERIMENTING AT STROH'S

What was I going to do? What I wanted to do was to follow my passion, to create my own signature brews. To do so, I would have to start my own commercial brewery. Unfortunately, Ontario's provincial bureaucrats informed me that they were not issuing any new brewery-sales licenses. I could buy a license from an existing licensee, but obviously there was no way a big brewer was going to sell one. I could obtain a federal brewing license, which would allow me to *brew* beer but not to *sell* it. (For that, I would need a provincial brewing license.)

In 1963, I obtained a federal license and set up my own pilot brewery in the basement of my home in Windsor, which was located on the Detroit River in southern Ontario.

I started out with a strain of yeast that I had first isolated in 1952, when I was assistant director of microbiological quality control at Canadian Breweries. Back then, I isolated pure cultures that were part of the brewery's mixed cultures of yeast that originally came from a brewery in the Midlands of central England, it was thought, and today would be almost two centuries old. From one compound yeast culture, I isolated about 14 single-celled pure yeast cultures, and then made a five-gallon batch of beer from each culture. I then selected the yeast that I thought made the best-flavored beer. I have continued to use that strain of yeast all these years. (It's the same yeast I use today to make Grant's Ales.)

At this time, I began doing experiments with a type of beer that effectively was the precursor to my Scottish Ale. I essentially was picking up where I left off at Canadian Breweries in the 1950s, when we were experimenting with the different hops and yeasts.

In the meantime, I had to make a living. Anheuser-Busch offered me a job, but I just couldn't see myself fitting into that kind of corporate life. And A-B, like most of the major breweries, had lost its traditions; the brewmasters were no longer running the show. Since I didn't respect the people who were running Labatt's, and Molson wasn't doing any research, my options were few.

Over the years, I would run into Peter Stroh—of the Stroh Brewing Company of Detroit—at brewing conferences, and we developed a very nice professional relationship. Back then, Stroh was a regional brewery, with distribution in Michigan, Indiana, Illinois, Ohio and West Virginia. I liked the Stroh's beer, called Bohemian, which Peter described as inspired by the beers produced in Pilsen. To my taste, Bohemian was the most distinctive of major-brand American beers, with enough hops to make you take notice.

In 1963, I drove down to Stroh to visit an old friend from Canadian Breweries, Jim McDougal, who was Stroh's quality-control chemist. We went out to lunch with Peter, who asked me to become Stroh's head of brewing development. I accepted. This seemed to me an ideal situation, because working in Detroit would allow me to continue to live in Windsor with my wife and four young children. Plus, Stroh also employed several other former Canadian Breweries colleagues of mine.

PETER STROH: WHY WE HIRED BERT

I was familiar with the pilot breweries that other brewing and malting companies had built, and I thought that having that capability was essential for any brewing company that aspired to technical excellence. We were searching for ways to make our beer better, to get a better understanding of the variables of the brewing process and how they affected our product.

Bert had been associated with Canadian Breweries' research director, Scotty MacFarlane, who put together one of the finest brewing labs that any of us were aware of. Canadian Breweries had well-trained brewers and strong support staff. That operation certainly served as a model for what I attempted to get for Stroh, and that's why we offered Bert the job.

As Stroh's "development chemist," I was, in effect, in charge of experimental brewing, mainly working on the quality control of Bohemian Beer. (For example, we tried out different methods of chill-proofing the beer.) I designed, built and programmed the pilot brewery, which could do up to eight different brews a day (usually four), seven gallons each, and I ran it four or five days a week. Of course, we had to sample all the results—boy, that involved a lot of tasting!

While working at Stroh, I gained an enormous amount of brewing experience and had great fun. I had the freedom to experiment with different adjuncts: different types of hops and high hop rates; different types of malt and mashing procedures; no-malt beers and malted wheat beers; sorghum and malted sorghum. (I never did get decent beer from sorghum.) My 100 percent malted rice beer was so bland, it would have suited the Budweiser people perfectly.

Stroh didn't create any new beer from the brews I developed, which was a source of profound frustration. At our weekly experimental brewery meetings, my samples were tasted by "The Big Panel" of marketers and senior brewers, who would invariably say, "Very nice, Bert, but we won't make it because it won't sell."

Thanks, But No Thanks

Stroh was an efficient, first-class operation with a beautiful bottling shop, and good packaging. Peter's uncle, John Stroh, who had become president and CEO in 1950 (the year the company turned 100), was the fourth generation of his family to run the brewery. John was a great leader. He walked through parts of the brewery every day—the cellar section one day; the fermenting section another day, and so on. If he found something wrong, he'd personally call the chief engineer and tell him to fix it. And if it wasn't fixed the next time John went through the brewery, there would be hell to pay.

Stroh was one of the first breweries to fully implement the process of centrifuging the fermented wort, instead of filtering it and letting it settle. George Stein helped me devise the process. At the end of fermentation, you can either chill the beer and let it sit for a couple of weeks to let the yeast settle out, or chill it and run it through a centrifuge. The latter takes nearly all the yeast out of the brew, saving settling time. Instead of having to scrape it off the bottom of the tank, you get the yeast out of the centrifuge in a compressed form (looking like toothpaste), which saves a lot of effort and, more importantly, a lot of beer. The yeast is in one place and can easily be used for the next brew. The rest of it can be added to the spent grains for cattle feed, or, if you're British, you can make it into Marmite, the stuff that the Brits spread on toast.

But as efficient as Stroh was, John Stroh was not an innovator. He was quite happy with the way things were and didn't want to make changes—not to his beer, anyway. I, on the other hand, was devoted to changing Stroh's brewing process: to make it less expensive to produce better beer.

For example, Stroh was one of the last U.S. breweries to use small, open, wooden fermenters. They had hundreds of them, each holding about 120 barrels, the equivalent of 3,720 gallons. Each brew had to go into eight or nine of these little wooden open fermenters. Every time they were going to be filled up, they first had to be scrubbed, cleaned and sterilized, which required a horrendous amount of manual labor and expense. Of course, the main trouble with wooden fermenters—even lined ones—is that they provide a hospitable breeding ground for all sorts of bacteria that can damage beer.

So, Peter Stroh and I came up with a scheme to replace the whole cellarful of little fermenters with a couple of large stainless steel tanks, which would have saved pots of money and, quite frankly, made more consistent beer. That idea was rejected—not just because of the up-front expense (even though its value would have been proved almost immediately), but mainly because it was too radical a change. As a proposal, it went way beyond the corporate comfort level.

PETER STROH ON BERT

As the quality advantages became increasingly apparent, we gradually produced more beer in horizontal, cylindrical tanks, and less and less in open wood fermenters. In the last years of the operation of our Detroit brewery, we had done what Bert had urged us to do 20 years before.

In retrospect, we didn't give Bert enough money to build a decent pilot brewery in the first place. I wish we had given him more to work with because, today, we attach an enormous amount of importance to our pilot brewing capability. We have first-rate facilities and skilled brewers working in those areas. But in the days when Bert was working for us, there was relatively little appreciation in our company of the importance of having a strong scientific and technical staff. We had wonderful master brewers and a rudimentary quality-control operation, but not much in between.

Hello, You're Fired

At least once a month, Peter, John and I would have lunch together to discuss the activities of the pilot brewery. One day in 1963, John's secretary called me and said I should be in his office by noon. I figured we were just meeting for lunch. I walked into his office and he said, "Bert, I've heard you're selling Stroh brewing secrets. You're fired."

He said that somebody had told him that I was a shareholder in a brewing consulting company—a company that I had never heard of. I later found out that this was a company that George Stein had set up. I wasn't aware of the fact that George had assigned me some shares, even though we had been consulting together.

Still, we weren't selling any Stroh's secrets. We had been consulting for a small start-up brewery in Canada that was interested in the technical process of continuous brewing that we had begun working on back in 1958-59 at Canadian Breweries. Canadian Breweries somehow learned of my involvement, and an executive there called his good friend John Stroh and voiced his displeasure.

My firing was a big shock for Peter Stroh, too. Peter, who remains my good friend to this day, describes that episode as "one of the most traumatic business messes that I can remember. We hated to see Bert leave."

But, to be honest with you, I wasn't unhappy getting fired. As always, new opportunities were right around the corner.

Examining the 1996 hop crop. As a member of the Hop Research Council during the late 1960s, I fought to "save" the Cascade hop. It's now one of America's most popular varieties.

Chapter Four

CONGRATULATIONS, YOU'RE A CONSULTANT

News travels fast in the beer business. By the time I got home after being fired from Stroh, I found five messages waiting for me. Four of them were job offers, including three from breweries in New York. Moving to New York was out of the question because it was not my favorite city. So, I did what any self-respecting canned brewer would do: I became a consultant. I formed International Brewing Consultants, and soon had several well-known clients, including Rheingold, Schaefer, Anheuser-Busch, Coors, Guinness, Foster's and S. S. Steiner, the world's second-largest hop company.

THE ANHEUSER-BUSCH PHILOSOPHY

After I left Stroh, Anheuser-Busch asked me to submit an application to be hired for their research department. I didn't bother to apply because I had spoken to friends of mine who were working there, and they told me that it was a rigid hierarchy. I didn't see much point in doing research there when there was no chance they would ever use any of it.

I sat in on a couple of taste tests with August Busch III. He knows the taste he wants in his beer, which is very bland. He doesn't want anything in it that stands out. That's one of the reasons why they've gone through so many different hopping procedures in the last 20 years. They have a taste that they want, and they don't want anything interfering with it, like a hop aroma. Their genius is in marketing and making a very well standardized beer. It's standardized at a very low flavor level, but it is standardized. I give them credit for consistency.

Since the 1950s, I had been doing experimental hop work with Steiner. When I ran the pilot brewery at Stroh, Tom Gimbel, who owned Steiner, was always coming up with different varieties and forms of hops and hop extracts. Steiner would send me a little block of a new variety of hops, which I brewed with and evaluated. So, when I left Stroh, I contacted Tom, who still wanted evaluations from a pilot brewery. I said, "Nobody at Stroh's wants to do the evaluation on your hop extracts. I've been doing all the work. Why don't you give me the contract?"

So, he did. Steiner helped me put together a pilot brewery and research lab in my basement in Windsor, where I made five-gallon batches of all kinds of experimental beers for Schaefer, Rheingold and other big breweries. I also consulted on new hop varieties, hop extracts and hop chemistry for many breweries.

SAVE THE CASCADES!

In the 1960s, during my consulting days, I was a member of the Hop Research Council—a group of growers and brewers that developed and tested new hop varieties, maybe 10 to 12 types per year. When I brewed with the sample of what later was called Cascade, I just loved the hops. I thought they were great, with a lovely citrus-floral note that was very different from the herbal character of most hops at the time.

But at the next meeting, the big brewers on the council said we should forget about Cascades—they didn't like the aroma, calling it excessively perfumy. I disagreed, and managed to persuade Peter Stroh to try using Cascades. Pretty soon, other brewers like Coors and even Anheuser-Busch changed their tune after they realized that you could boil off the Cascade aroma and still retain the hops' "pleasant bitterness." In 1972, the Cascade hop was officially introduced into production.

Today, thanks to the very floral aroma that the major breweries found objectionable, Cascade is the most recognizable and most famous Northwest hop variety. Perhaps more than any other variety, Cascades are emblematic of America's new wave of ales, particularly those on the West Coast. They are used exclusively in my flagship Scottish Ale, and are prominent in beers like Sierra Nevada Pale Ale and Anchor Liberty Ale.

And on a side note, it was my experiments with Cascades that started me on the path to inventing isomerized hop pellets—but that's another story . . .

One of my favorite clients was Guinness. On one of my first trips to Ireland to visit Guinness, in the 1950s, the company was rebuilding its black-malt facility—where barley is roasted to achieve a coffee-like character—which had just burned down. They told me that was no big deal; their black-malt facility burnt to the ground every decade or so. This visit also provided me with a "research" opportunity—taking in the Thursday night "Pub Crawls" in neighboring Edinburgh, Scotland, with my cousin, Jock Stuart. Jock, who grew barley for whiskey, could drink single malt the way most people drink beer. His typical breakfast consisted of 10 ounces of single-malt scotch and a bowl of porridge.

Having my own pilot brewery was liberating. I could try whatever I wanted, I didn't have to get approval from some committee, I retained ownership of my own discoveries, and I was free to experiment with new processes, such as continuous brewing.

Bert Grant's Brewery

1. Dry Grain Storage

Beer can be made from any grain, but barley is the variety of choice for brewers. After being harvested, barley is "malted"—steeped in water until it starts to sprout, then quickly dried over hot air. (Depending on the duration and intensity of heat, the barley malt can range from a pale to toasted, brown, or black color and character.) The malting process allows the barley's starch to be converted to sugar during the brewing process. We keep our pale barley malt—the base for all my Grant's Ales—in a grain silo outside the brewery. Inside, we store bags of "specialty" malts (including some of the darker-roasted varieties) that are used to give each brew a distinctive character. We also use malted wheat, in addition to barley, to brew Grant's HefeWeizen.

2. Malt Mill

The malt storage is conveniently located next to the malt mill. Before brewing, we crush all the malt in the mill: the process cracks open the hard husk around each barley kernel, exposing the starch inside. The key is to crush the grain rather than to shatter it, as the malt husks later will help clarify the pre-beer at the end of the "mashing" process.

3. Grain Elevator

The crushed malt is carried via a grain elevator to the top of the tower brewery. Before the 20th century, breweries historically were built on a tower system, which uses gravity to enable the flow from vessel to vessel during the brewing process. Today we know that, by eliminating the need to pump liquid from vessel to vessel, the tower system actually enhances beer quality: pumps can break up grain husks, slowing down runoff into the brewkettle (and imparting grainier flavors to beer). More important, pumps can break up protein "chains" created in the brewkettle, causing hazy beer down the line. A gravity-fed tower brewhouse makes better-quality beer while preserving tradition.

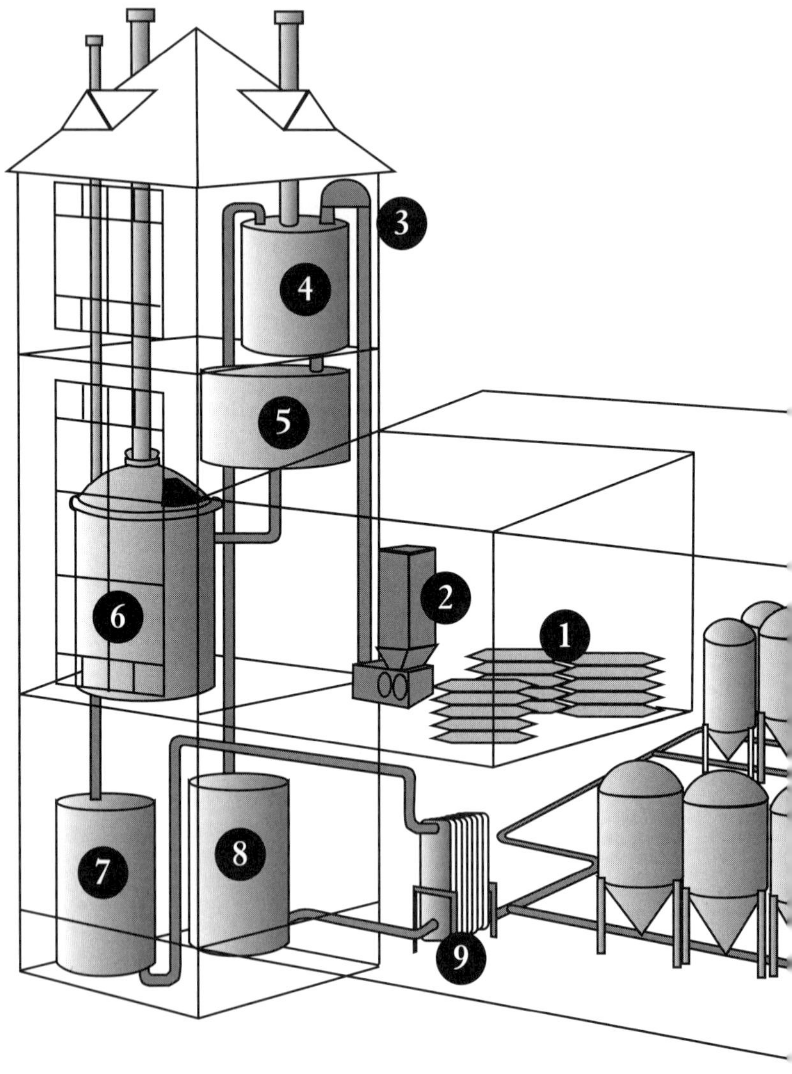
1
2
3
4
5
6
7
8
9

BERT GRANT'S BREWERY, YAKIMA, WA.

1. Dry Grain Storage
2. Malt Mill
3. Grain Elevator
4. Mash Tun
5. Lauter Tun
6. Brewkettle
7. Hot Wort Tank
8. Hot Liquor Tank
9. Heat Exchanger
10. Fermenters
11. Filtration Unit
12. Bright Beer Tanks
13. Packaging Equipment
14. Cold Storage

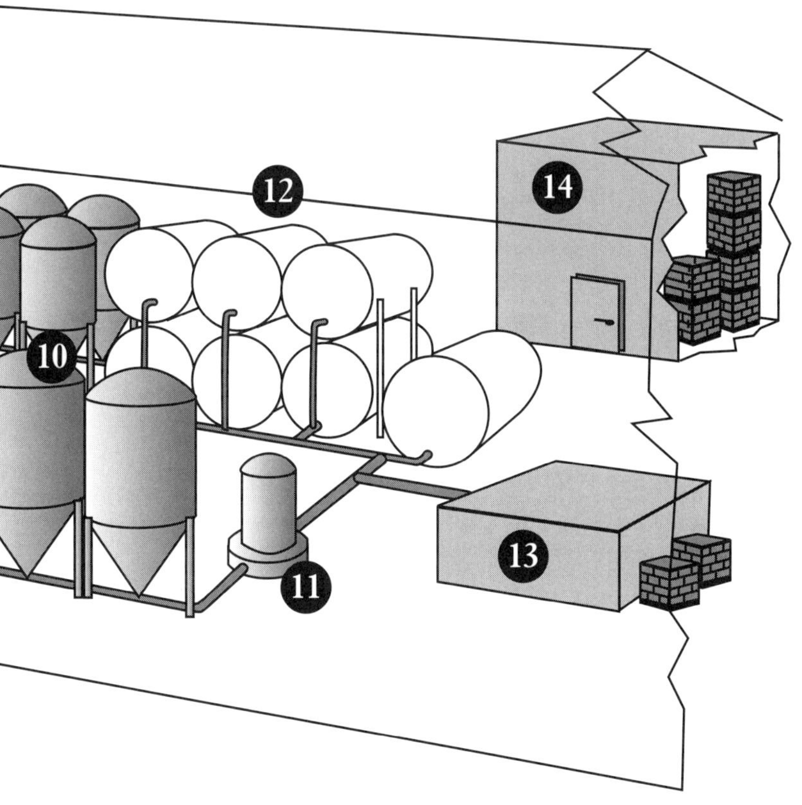

4. Mash Tun

In this vessel (or "tun"), the crushed grain mixes with hot (but not boiling) water—literally brewing, just like coffee or tea is "brewed" by being steeped in hot water. The resulting porridge-like mixture is called "the mash." During this process, which usually lasts for about an hour and a half, natural barley enzymes convert the grain starch to sugar. Flavors and color from specialty grains also are absorbed into the liquid.

5. Lauter Tun

After mashing is complete, the grain-and-water mixture is drained into the lauter tun (a vessel whose name comes from the German verb meaning "to clarify"). A perforated "false" bottom in the lauter tun allows the sugary-sweet "barley water" to drain into the brewkettle (6) while the grain husks stay behind. This sugary liquid is called wort (pronounced "wert"), and the remaining material is referred to as "spent grain." As the wort flows out, hot water is sprayed over the top of the grain to ensure that every possible bit of sugar is extracted. Finally, the spent grain is deposited into a container and sold to local farmers as cattle feed.

6. Brewkettle

The wort drains from the lauter tun into the brewkettle, where I add my trademark hops. The brewkettle is used to boil the wort for two reasons: first, to sterilize it prior to fermentation; second, to allow certain hop compounds (which provide bitterness, balancing the wort's malty sweetness) to be absorbed into the beer. The point at which the hops are added—toward the beginning or end of the boil, for example—affects which of their aspects (bitterness, aroma, flavor) will be emphasized in the finished beer. My brewkettle is made from copper (an excellent conductor of heat) and fired by a direct flame. The direct-fired process creates a vigorous, rolling boil in the kettle (which enhances beer quality) and also imparts some pleasing caramelized flavors to the beer (a result of hot spots created where the flame strikes the kettle). Copper also provides essential nutrients needed by yeast during fermentation.

7. Hot Wort Tank

After the boil, the hopped wort drains into this receiving vessel. It flows in at an angle, creating a "whirlpool" effect that forces coagulated material (created during the boil) and any leftover hop or grain residue to settle out in the bottom, center of the tank – where they are easily removed. The end result: relatively clear wort prior to fermentation. The hopped wort then runs from here to the heat exchanger (9).

8. Hot Liquor Tank

In brewer-speak, water used during the mash is called "liquor." This vessel is a storage tank to ensure that enough hot water is available to perform the mash. In addition to having its own heater, the tank collects hot water from the heat exchanger (9).

9. Heat Exchanger

This radiator-like device is used to cool the hopped wort to a temperature at which yeast can survive and thrive, fermenting the wort into beer. Cold water runs on one side of a thin metal strip, hot wort on the other, and they "exchange" heat: the wort is cooled down (to approximately 70 degrees F), the water warmed up (and then collected in the hot liquor tank).

10. Fermenters

Once the wort fills a fermenter, yeast is added to start fermentation. The process is straightforward: a yeast cell "eats" a molecule of sugar and, as its by-products, gives off alcohol and carbon dioxide (fizz!). We use a unique "ale yeast" to ferment Grant's beers. This yeast works at relatively warm "ale" temperatures (around 70 degrees F)—each fermenter is individually controlled to ensure optimal temperature—and imparts distinctive, fruity flavors and aromas to the finished beer. (Lager yeasts, by comparison, work at cooler temperatures and tend to impart far fewer flavor and aroma compounds.) Our standard fermentation process takes about a week.

11. Filtration Unit

Following fermentation, the beer is filtered to remove any leftover solids (including yeast) that have made it through the whole process. (The one exception obviously is Grant's HefeWeizen, in which unfiltered yeast is meant to remain in the keg and bottle.) Filtration also helps improve the beer's stability—but too "tight" a filtration, such as the micro-filters used by many big breweries, can strip a beer of body and character. We go to great lengths to get the balance just right.

12. Bright Beer Tanks

Following fermentation, the filtered (or "bright," in brewer-speak) beer is matured in these tanks for a few days—allowing its flavors to meld together—prior to bottling or kegging.

13. Packaging Equipment

The beer runs from the bright tanks into the bottling or kegging lines, where it is packaged for sale. Grant's line isn't as flashy or fast as the football-field-sized versions at big breweries, but it works just as well: the beer goes into bottles and kegs with a minimum of oxygen exposure (which damages flavor), and at the peak of freshness. We even use brown-glass bottles to give Grant's Ales maximum protection against damaging light exposure (which causes "skunky" aromas).

14. Cold Storage

After packaging, our beer is either immediately shipped out for sale (in refrigerated trucks) or briefly put into our cold storage warehouse. Cool temperatures preserve the beer's fresh flavor, ensuring that it remains in top condition until it is shipped to retailers. You can taste the results every time you enjoy a distinctive Bert Grant's Ale!

Continuous Brewing System

Outside of the experiments we'd done at Canadian Breweries, the pilot brewery in my basement was probably the first continuous brewing and fermentation operation in North America. It was very small, but it was the first to integrate both continuous brewing and continuous fermentation.

Traditional brewing is a batch process. You make a certain amount of wort—say 100 barrels' worth—in the mash cooker, then separate it from the spent grain in the lauter tun, then boil it with hops in the brewkettle, cool it and ferment it. At the end, you have around 100 barrels of finished beer.

In my idea for the continuous brewing system, you shred up the hops and mix them with the wort as it comes out of the lauter tun. Instead of being boiled (for an hour or more) in the kettle, the hopped wort runs into a heat exchanger, where it is compressed under pressure and flash-heated to around 140 degrees Celsius. Then it shoots out into a big tank, where it expands and vents a whole bunch of steam (blowing off all the undesirables that usually go up the smokestack during a traditional boil).

You're left with perfectly hopped wort, ready for fermentation, in much less time than the traditional manner. You also avoid some of the "stewed" flavors that sometimes can develop in the brewkettle if you're not careful.

BARRELS, KEGS AND PINTS—OH, MY!

The definition of a "brewer's barrel," the standard measure of production in the American beer industry, actually comes from those big wooden barrels that brewery deliverymen used to cart in and out of taverns. The standard "barrel" held 31 gallons (US) of beer. Today's standard "keg" size is technically a half-barrel (15.5 gallons, or about 120 pints). A "pony keg" is a quarter-barrel. One-sixth barrels (a little more than five gallons) are gaining in popularity among brewers and tavern owners because of their convenient smaller size.

The only trouble is that a lot of protein-based clogs would build up in the heat exchanger. To address this, we built a duplicate "hot section." We would use the first hot section for three to six hours, shut it down, and switch to the second hot section and run that one for three to six hours. Meanwhile, we would caustic-wash the first so it would be clean, sterilized and ready to go when we made the switch. That's what made much of the operation virtually continuous.

The next step, of course, was continuous fermentation. In the traditional brewing process, the batch of wort (about 100 barrels) would run into a suitably sized tank and ferment into beer over about seven days.

In the continuous fermentation system, things were a little different. The hopped wort enters one of two tanks arranged in series, flowing in at a continuous rate (say, a half-barrel per minute). Inside this tank, an extremely vigorous fermentation is going on—so vigorous, in fact, that "pre-beer" is flowing out of the tank as fast as it's entering (a half-barrel per minute). It comes in, ferments down about two-thirds of the way almost "instantly" (with some help from dilution), and you've got this partially fermented beer flowing out to another tank at the same rate.

In the second tank, the same process happens, with fermentation going to completion. So you've got fully fermented, young beer flowing out of this tank at the same rate—a half-barrel per minute—into an aging tank (before bottling, kegging, etc.). To ferment our 100 barrels, then, it would take a little over three hours (maybe two days when you add aging time)—compared to seven days in the traditional scheme. Plus, you don't need a big 100-barrel tank; you can get by with two much smaller tanks.

Best of all, continuous fermentation enhances beer quality. The fermentation is so vigorous, with such a high concentration of active yeast, that it's almost impossible for any bacteria or other "bugs" to take hold in the beer. Additionally, because of the intense yeast activity, you don't get any of the off-flavors that sometimes come during fermentation. In fact, with lager beers, you get much less of the sulfur character that can develop in a normal batch.

But here's the catch: *in a small brewery that makes a range of different beer styles (all with different recipes), continuous brewing doesn't really offer any benefits.* That's why we don't use the system to make Grant's Ales today; we still brew each batch individually by hand. At a larger brewery making substantial amounts of a single beer (similar to what we were doing at Canadian Breweries), however, the value of continuous brewing can be enormous.

Unfortunately, big breweries didn't see the advantage of this system. The ones that tried it made such basic engineering and microbiological mistakes that the process was doomed to failure. Our test program at Canadian Breweries failed for a much more mundane reason: responding to internal politics, the company built our continuous brewing facility in Montreal and our continuous fermentation plant in Toronto. Almost all efficiency was lost. Now that's corporate thinking at its finest!

Business Lessons The Hard Way

In the early 1960s, George Stein, who sold centrifuges to Canadian Breweries' O'Keefe operation, worked with me on the idea of making this continuous brewing operation into a business. George and I put together a plan for a million-barrel plant that would cost $5 to $10 million—a fifth of the cost of a conventional brewery. We tried selling our idea to people in countries all over the world to show them they could afford to build their own breweries.

There was just one hitch: we didn't have an active brewery to prove that our system worked.

Although we didn't want to be in the brewery business, we had no choice. Getting a new license in Ontario was virtually impossible because of the province's archaic laws. So, we had to find a brewery that was already running and was available at a reasonable price. We raised a couple of hundred thousand dollars and found one in Fort Frances, Ontario, which is on the border of International Falls, Minnesota.

In the meantime, George met a representative of a large supermarket chain from the Midwest, and got to talking about the possibility of his company having a house brand of imported Canadian beer. The guy thought that was a marvelous idea. Their distribution center was in Minneapolis, so it would have been an easy truck drive from Fort Frances.

We checked out the Fort Frances plant, inventoried the equipment, looked at the books and put together a financial proposal. We saw that we could easily convert this plant to a continuous brewing operation and ship the production into the States, and eventually expand into the Toronto market. Most important, we would then have an operating plant to show potential clients that it could be done.

But right before we could make our offer to the brewery's owner, he informed us that he had sold it to another party—a promoter who put down a few thousand dollars for an option. In short order, the promoter peddled stock in the brewery, collected the money and then disappeared! After the stock fraud blew over, the owner of the brewery offered to sell it to us. But our financial backers were no longer interested because the brewery was connected with a fraud. So much for *that* plan.

The continuous brewing process, however, lives on. It was later used (with reasonable success) in England, and is still in use in breweries in Australia and New Zealand. (Too bad they can't make better beer.) Thirty-five years later, my theory is finally catching on. I liked being ahead of the crowd, but it's a lonely place. I've learned that the trick is to be slightly in the lead—not miles ahead of everyone else in the race.

IT'S AUSTRALIAN FOR "MONOPOLY"

Back in the 1960s, Foster's had a total lock on the Australian beer market. It seemed as if any pub they didn't own, they had a mortgage on. That's why I was not impressed with the Aussies coming to international beer industry meetings and telling us what great beer they made because they sold so much of it. "Well, you sell an awful lot of beer to thirsty people who can't buy anything else," I kept pointing out. It was the same with the big brewers in New Zealand. They had a monopoly.

HOP CAPITAL OF NORTH AMERICA

Washington's Yakima Valley grows around 75 percent of the country's annual crop and is known as America's "hop heartland." Where better to build my brewery?

Chapter Five

WHERE IN THE WORLD IS YAKIMA, WASHINGTON?

As you might imagine, this was a deeply frustrating time of my life. Fortunately, I had a lot of interesting prospects.

In 1967, S. S. Steiner asked me to design a hop-extract plant for construction near its headquarters in Yakima, in south-central Washington State. Hop extracts are to hops what bouillon cubes are to soup—they get the job done, providing bitterness to beer, but with none of the romance (or hassle, from a big brewer's perspective) of working with whole hop cones. And back in the late 1960s, when good, consistent hop pellets were still a few years away, hop extracts were the popular alternative.

HOPPING IN KENT, WASHINGTON

Before Yakima became famous for its hops, the center of Washington State hop-growing was the town of Kent, which was named after the county in England that was the hop-growing center of the U.K. That was before a blight killed the crop. Now, only remnants of hops grow up telephone poles and fence posts.

Yakima is the hub of the fertile Yakima Valley, which is the center of U.S. hop production and the most prolific hop-growing region in the world. Earlier in this century, French-Canadian immigrants from Quebec settled in Yakima, and started planting hops because they needed a crop to grow. With its long, hot summer days, the valley is blessed with an ideal hops-growing climate. It produces an extremely reliable crop—including more than 15 different varieties—that is purchased by most of the world's top breweries. (It accounts for about 30 percent of the world hop market.) The valley also is known for its lush orchards of fruit, from apples to grapes. There are certain spots in the valley where you can see a hop field standing next to an apple orchard across from a vineyard!

After I submitted my design for the new plant, Steiner instead opted to buy into an existing Yakima Valley extract plant, and the company owner, Tom Gimbel, asked me to become the plant's technical director. At that time, I had no intention of moving to Yakima—or anywhere else—and the last thing I wanted was to go back to being a full-time employee for a big company.

On the other hand, I knew I'd be working directly for Tom Gimbel, reporting right "to the top," so I agreed—*reluctantly*—to take the job. Although my wife and kids were adamantly against it, we moved to Yakima in 1967. It was something of a family trauma, and I always felt guilty about it. But it was a decision I felt that I had to make.

My Patented Pellets

The problem with whole hop cones, once they've been dried and baled after harvest, is that they lose their aroma and bittering value over time—even during the space of one year. So you have to retest and readjust your recipes if you're brewing with whole hops on an ongoing basis, in order to get consistent character in the finished beer. You also have to deal with the fact that your bittering values may vary from batch to batch of whole cones.

Around the 1950s, some bright spark in Germany came up with the idea of pulverizing hops and extruding them in pellet form (they look a little like rabbit food). This gave hops an improved storage life—since less of their surface area was exposed to air, compared to whole cones—and also provided a reliable, known bittering value in every batch.

In 1972, I helped Steiner build the first hop-pellet plant in the Yakima Valley, and, for that matter, the U.S. I also came up with a patented process for creating "isomerized" pellets, which can provide bitterness to beer without the need for a lengthy boil in the brewkettle. Nobody had ever thought about doing this before. Today, in some countries such as South Africa, brewers use only isomerized pellets. In America, 20 percent of the beer is made with isomerized pellets.

In addition, while working at Steiner, we discovered that prolonged storage of pellets—a year or two—resulted in some loss of aroma and bittering ability. I devised another patented process to stabilize pellets by mixing food-grade magnesium oxide with the pulverized hop powder prior to pelletizing. Today, to preserve the hops as well as possible, pellets are packaged in vacuum-sealed bags.

The extract plant Steiner bought was underutilized, inefficient and poorly designed. Immediately after its acquisition, I improved the design and quickly tripled its efficiency.

I remained technical director at Steiner's extract plant from 1967 to 1972. In 1972, I oversaw the building of a new processing plant for pellets—which was not only the first in the U.S. but was also at one time the largest in the world, processing 6 million pounds a year. My time at Steiner was satisfying; the work was challenging and fun. But by the early 1980s, I saw that there really wasn't much more for me to do, except to produce pellets and convince breweries to use them.

I was at the point where I wanted to do something else. But I was living in Yakima, known more for fresh fruit than fresh ideas, and, at age 50, I was at a point in life when most people plan for retirement, not dreaming up a new business. Surprisingly, this was the time I chose to come up with an idea that helped transform an industry.

Celebrating the expansion of our pioneering Brewery Pub in 1983 (l to r): a Seattle journalist chats with me, John Stroh II (visiting from Michigan), and Rick Desmarais.

Chapter Six

A DREAM COME TRUE: GRANT'S ALES

In March of 1981, the Yakima chapter of the Enological Society, an organization dedicated to the study of wine and other fermented beverages, hosted a beer-tasting conducted by a beer-importing firm based in Seattle. For me, this would be a fateful event.

The presenter offered some very interesting Belgian beers and British beers. But I was teed off by her negative attitude about American beers such as Budweiser and Miller. What particularly bothered me was when she said that all American beers use 160 different chemicals. Nonsense. Maybe 160 chemicals were *approved* for use, but no brewery uses more than two or three. Her line of reasoning should have been that people should pay the extra money for imports because they taste better, not because Budweiser is made from chemicals—it isn't. I told the Enological Society that *I* would host the next tasting and set the record straight on beer—both domestic and imported.

MY FAVORITE INTERNATIONAL CITIES

The first city that comes to mind is Prague. The Czech Republic has great lager beers. Some of the draft in Prague is just marvelous. It's great stuff. If you had one place to go for the best lager, it would be Prague. There is a place called The Clock, which serves very good Pilsner Urquell.

If you just want to drink volumes of good beer, any of the beer halls in Munich would be satisfactory.

Edinburgh is one of the world's greatest brewing cities, with lots of pubs serving high-quality, cask-conditioned beer. I've been lucky enough to never get a bad pint there.

Six months later, in September 1981, I ran a proper tasting for about 90 members of the Enological Society at the Women's Century Club in Yakima. I started off with Budweiser and Miller—very light beers; then Henry Weinhard (which at the time was still a regional Northwest brand); then a couple of more substantial imported stouts—Courage Imperial Russian Stout and the classic Guinness dry stout. The last two beers in the tasting were two of my own beers—Scottish Ale and Imperial Stout.

The reaction was overwhelming. Several people said they'd buy the beer if it was commercially available. More important, before the evening was out, a dentist named Bill Harrison and a doctor named Eric Benson said that they would become investors if I ever wanted to build my own brewery. Now that's a vote of confidence!

INSPIRATIONS: ANCHOR STEAM AND SIERRA NEVADA

By the early 1980s, there were only two American breweries making "real," gutsy beer—the Anchor Brewing Co. of San Francisco and Sierra Nevada Brewery of Chico, California.

In 1965, Fritz Maytag purchased Anchor, which had once been a major brewer but had come upon hard times. I was in their original plant—actually a combination of three big run-down breweries—right after Fritz bought it. It was the worst mess I'd ever seen, with broken windows that allowed pigeons to fly in and drop their "calling card." Fritz Maytag received a tremendous amount of help from the local San Francisco independent brewmasters, including the people at Lucky Lager, who gave him some equipment. Now, Fritz is still there and they are all gone.

Anchor produces its distinctive Anchor Steam Beer through a unique process that involves fermentation with a lager yeast at higher "ale" temperatures. This creates a very effervescent beer. When the beer was tapped from old wooden barrels, the story goes, it hissed out in a spray, so people started calling it "steam beer."

In 1981, I read an article in Brewers Digest *about the opening of Sierra Nevada, so I went down to Chico to see it. I had a nice chat with Ken Grossman, who started Sierra Nevada, and he showed me this tiny garage-type operation that he put together with his original partner Paul Camusi after nearly two years of study and research. Ken is a very clever engineer.*

The Sierra Nevada Pale Ale was good beer from day one. I tried to talk Ken into using pelletized hops, but he preferred to brew the beer in a totally traditional manner, including the use of whole hops. Anytime I'm in Northern California, I visit their marvelous operation; it's just beautiful. I think Sierra Pale Ale and Grant's Scottish Ale are the two most consistent beers produced since the start of the whole craft-beer movement.

Yakima Brewing & Malting Co.

Well, of course I wanted to build my own brewery. In recent years, new microbreweries have attracted investors with a glossy prospectus, a sophisticated business plan, an exhaustive market study and the optimistic projected numbers to justify the investment. We had none of that. I put in $30,000 of my own money and joined up with a dozen other investors to form the Yakima Brewing & Malting Co. (I owned about 60 percent of the company.) Despite the investment, which was a significant amount for me, I saw the brewery as a hobby. I still kept my job at Steiner.

A local developer heard that we were looking for a brewery site and took us to 25 N. Front Street, where he was renovating the old Yakima Transfer & Storage building. It was across the street from an active railroad station in a seedy downtown area that had been one step away from the wrecking ball. When the pool hall and the house of ill repute moved in next door, that was considered a neighborhood improvement!

Although in a ramshackle condition when we looked at it, the building boasted a colorful history, beginning its life at the end of the 19th century as Yakima's opera house. In 1900, it became the site of the North Yakima Brewing and Malting Co. and saloon, remaining in business until the voters of Washington—obviously laboring under gross misconceptions—made the state dry in 1917.

The Sorry State of Mega Brewing

The number of breweries in the U.S. reached a peak of almost 2,000 at the beginning of the 20th century. From then on, the total steadily dwindled, for a variety of reasons, most notably Prohibition, which went into effect in 1920. In 1934, a year after Prohibition was repealed, there were 750 operating breweries in the U.S.

The surviving companies stopped brewing unique, fuller-flavored beers in favor of brands with "broader" appeal. With the rise of national marketing, advertising and distribution in the 1950s—and the intensification of price competition—major companies dramatically increased their individual brewing capacities, in some cases as high as 19 million barrels per year. By contrast, today, the Coors Brewery in Golden, Colorado—the largest single-site brewery in the world—alone produces 20 million barrels per year.

At the same time, they took shortcuts in the brewing process, lowered ingredient costs and malt ratios, and diluted the product. The average hop flavor, as measured by "bitterness units," declined from 20 parts per million in the 1950s to 12 parts per million in the 1970s. Mainstream beer could not be distinguished by sensory analyses, only by the labels.

Major brewers also eliminated minor brands because they complicated production schedules and diluted advertising budgets. By the early 1980s, there were only 99 licensed breweries in America, producing almost 177 million barrels of beer. Almost half of these were branch plants of the six largest breweries, which accounted for over 90 percent of beer production in the U.S. No wonder beer drinkers were thirsty for change! By 1998, as a result of America's craft-beer revolution, there were more than 1,300 breweries, including brewpubs—a victory for good beer.

August Busch III admitted to Fortune *magazine in 1997, "If you had asked us 10 years ago whether there would be X-hundred little tiny brewers across this country who will end up with 3 percent of the market and 6 percent of the margin pool, we would've said no. . . . We were five years late in recognizing that they were going to take as much market as they did and five years late in recognizing we should have joined them."*

We could see immediately that it needed a lot of work, but it was obviously a diamond in the rough, with wonderful potential as a brewery. It had large front windows and arched doors and, most important, it already contained a refrigerated vault that had once provided summer refuge for most of the ladies' fur coats in Yakima. Where better, I thought, for a fermenting and storage room? We signed a lease in January 1982, and ultimately spent $100,000 turning the building back into a brewery.

Our brewhouse, which was visible from the street via a large storefront-type window, was a grown-up version of my pilot breweries. It consisted of the mash/lauter tun and a direct-fire copper brewkettle (with a five-barrel—155-gallon—batch capacity) that was made to my design specifications by a local fabricator. We had four fermenters and an annual capacity of only 1,000 barrels. Rick Desmarais, our original brewer and production manager, came to work for me after five years as a laboratory technician at S. S. Steiner. He also helped me build the malt mill.

DIRECT-FIRED COPPER KETTLE

Traditionally, brewkettles were made of copper because they were fired over an open flame and because copper is an excellent conductor of heat. In the classic fashion, we've always used a direct-fired copper kettle. (We use American copper, fabricated in Tennessee by the same company that makes whiskey stills.)

We get even heat, which spreads quickly across the kettle. If we have a few hot spots, they just enhance caramelization in the kettle (and add to the character of our beer). Although it is difficult to prove definitively, I feel that direct-fire brewing is superior to other methods because it gives you much more even heat, and brings out a little more of our distinctive caramel flavor.

In recent years, brewers have discovered that copper actually provides an essential yeast nutrient that is important during fermentation. In an all-stainless-steel brewhouse, the yeast will eventually show signs of starvation, which happened to a few breweries back in the late 1950s and early 1960s.

Anheuser-Busch plants are almost entirely stainless steel, except for one big copper pipe that transports the wort. That's just enough copper for the yeast.

SCOTTISH ALE

As I said, at the time we first fired up our copper kettle, we didn't do any marketing surveys. I just decided to make beer that I liked and hoped that other people would like it, too. Over the years, we've introduced beers that complemented our line, and we knew they would find a market of their own.

Scottish Ale was the obvious first choice because it was my favorite home-brewed beer style—and has been my favorite beer since 1945, when I first tasted Dominion White Label ale at Canadian Breweries. The emigrant Scottish brewmasters who made Dominion White Label assured me that I was tasting the same kind of ales that were brewed in Scotland. That was my reference. It wasn't that I was tasting imported beers, which were extremely rare in those days in Ontario. When I got older, I visited Scotland and tasted the ales there myself. *Heaven.*

I knew exactly what I wanted to make: all-malt, intensely hopped, naturally conditioned Scottish Ale that would be as close as possible to Dominion White Label.

The yeast was from the National Yeast Culture collection in Norfolk, England. I had selected it, in the 1970s, from more than two dozen strains suggested by the supervisors of the collection, including several that I had archived there during my work for Canadian Breweries. The strain I ultimately selected was one that I had isolated in 1954 from a multi-strain culture that originated at a brewery in the English Midlands.

At the time, we were one of a handful of U.S. breweries using true top-fermenting ale yeast. Today there are a lot of ale-breweries in America. But our yeast gives you a really distinctive "ale" character: lots of fruity esters and other flavors. I want people to know they're drinking a true ale.

YEAST

An active yeast is a happy yeast. *If you keep the yeast strong and vigorous—by continually brewing with it—you never have to replace it. You must keep yeast fed with nutritious wort.*

One of the worst mistakes a brewer can make is to buy yeast commercially whenever you need it, as opposed to keeping your own pure supply. That's what Redhook did in the beginning. They got some absolutely wild yeast, from Belgium or some such place, and tried to make English ale with it. The beer was all over the bloody map. Their early "banana beer" was all funky, but some was worse. You never knew what you were going to get when you ordered a Redhook in the early days.

By comparison, Budweiser yeast is carefully controlled. They ship fresh yeast to all the breweries from St. Louis. Bud brewers all over the country are instructed in how to get started, into the tank, how long to leave it in the tank, when to take it out, how many brews they can use it for. Then, they get a new batch from St. Louis.

Traditionally, ale brewers didn't think it was possible to have one pure yeast strain. They thought you needed a big mixture of yeasts to get the proper ale flavor. But if one or two of the strains get ahead of the others, you have a different product.

The rest of the ingredients were local. The water came from the snowpack runoff in Washington State's Cascade Mountains (which separate Yakima and eastern Washington from Puget Sound to the west). The hops were Yakima Valley Cascades (the finest aromatic hops in the world), added at a rate at least three times that of any of the major U.S. lagers. The bitterness units were about 40 to 45, which is where I think it should be. For some people, it was too bitter. If they didn't like it, well, there was plenty of other beer out there to drink.

Our premium Northwest two-row barley was malted to the highest specifications by Great Western Malting Company in Vancouver, Washington. We were using approximately double the malt-per-barrel of beer brewed that domestic breweries used. Unlike today, at that time you couldn't buy small amounts of specialty malts—it was train-car loads or nothing. So, we rigged up a system to roast about 5 percent of the malt ourselves, using it to achieve our signature copper color in Scottish Ale. That's why we put "Malting Company" in our name.

The Scottish Ale that we brewed in our five-barrel kettle was marvelous. It should have been; I'd been working on versions of it since the 1950s, when I ran the pilot brewery at Canadian Breweries, and I continued making batches for my own consumption in the pilot brewery I had in the basement of my Windsor home.

ROGER PROTZ ON BERT

Roger Protz edits What's Brewing *(the monthly newspaper of Britain's Campaign for Real Ale) and is the author of several books such as* The Ale Trail, Classic Porter & Stout *and* The Ultimate Encyclopedia of Beer.

"There are two great pioneers in the industry," says Protz. "One is Fritz Maytag and the other one is Bert Grant. People talk about the great explosion of microbreweries in the late '80s and early '90s. Those two guys have been doing it for a lot longer than that. When it seemed that the big breweries would just get bigger and bigger and bigger, and the beers would get blander and blander and blander, they were going against the grain. Bert had the early advantage of combining a technical expertise with a passion for the product."

It was perfect beer, as far as I was concerned. There's not much to discuss about it. This is the best ale in the world. Very well balanced, with lovely caramel malt, butterscotch, a lot of hop aroma and bitterness. Some people may think it's too malty; some people may think it's too hoppy. But to my taste, it's just the right balance.

When you first take a sip of a proper ale, you should get a mouthful of texture, not just water. Commercial brewers who make Scottish ale usually make it much too watery, without enough body or bitterness. Our Cascade hops give it just the right amount of hoppy bitterness; with 40-plus bitterness units, you get a strong flavor impact from the hops. Finally, as Grant's Scottish Ale goes down your throat, you get a distinct butterscotch character—a traditional note in both classic English and Scottish ales.

Our first commercial batch tasted exactly as it did in the pilot brewery. Talk about exciting! That moment was nothing less than the highlight of my career and the realization of a four-decade dream.

It was especially nice to see that so many people liked my Scottish Ale. Over the years, all the brewing people I had given samples to said, "Oh, it's very tasty, Bert. I like it, but I don't think the public will like it." I didn't have to have the whole public like it. All I had to do was get one percent of the public liking it.

Those of us at the brewery certainly liked it. We analyzed it very carefully. Since we didn't have any fancy lab equipment, we relied on "sensory evaluation"—i.e., drinking it ourselves. Occasionally, we ended up "over-analyzing" the beer—strictly in the name of research, of course.

The "working ladies" in the brothel next door to the brewery used to hang out at the loading dock to get free samples. I always wondered if Scottish Ale worked as part of the barter system, but I was too busy brewing to ever get a chance to find out.

Grant's Scottish Ale has a higher alcohol content (4.7 percent by volume) than the common ales of Scotland, but doesn't taste as heavy as a typical strong Scottish ale. If it's going to be your everyday beer, you don't want something approaching a malt liquor or barley wine. If you went to Scotland to order a beer like this, you'd ask for "80-shilling, cask conditioned"—although it wouldn't have the Cascade hop character that is in our beer.

In fact, I want to reiterate one thing: Grant's Scottish Ale is based on my interpretation of the kind of beers—such as Dominion White Label—that the Scottish brewmasters at Canadian Breweries were making back in the 1940s. Sure, it has a malt character comparable to the Scottish 80-shilling ale style. But indigenous Scottish ales in general are much sweeter in character, thanks to Scotland's damp climate (which is suited for growing barley, not hops). As I indicate right on its label, Grant's Scottish is malty "in the tradition of Scotland" but also "hoppy in the tradition of Yakima." I originally named it "Scottish" because I was born in Scotland—that's all, plain and simple.

Cask Conditioning

When I first walked into a pub in Scotland in the 1950s and tasted authentic cask-conditioned ale, I felt I had died and gone to heaven. To this day, I prefer drinking cask-conditioned ale in a pub for one simple reason: ale tastes best—and has the best aroma—when it's just finished fermenting.

With cask-conditioning, you put the beer in the barrel or "cask" for its final fermentation. Because there is no extraneous pressure in the keg—beyond what CO2 remains naturally in the beer after it completes fermentation—you get a low-carbonated beer that is strong in fruity esters.

The problem is that the optimum flavor lasts for only a few days once the cask is tapped, and then it's a different beer. That's why I like drinking fresh cask-conditioned beer at our Brewery Pub. Quite often, I'll ask the bartender in our pub how the cask is pouring, and he'll say, "It's pretty good today. It was better yesterday."

One of the projects I'm going to seriously get into one of these days is to get cask-conditioned flavor in the bottle. I tried it in the '60s when I had my pilot brewery, but it didn't keep very well. Bottle-conditioned beers perhaps come closest, but even they don't really capture it. I've got theories on how I can do it.

Scottish Ale is a good all-around ale. I drink a pint or two every day. It's my favorite because it's the most satisfying. When you have a bottle of this, you know you've had a beer. I love it with Stilton or the strong white English cheddar cheese I grew up with in Ontario. It's good with shiskebob, spaghetti and seafood.

What's a Microbrew?

Although they didn't use the term "microbrewing," hundreds of years ago craftsmen engaged in small-scale "hearth brewing" or "kitchen brewing" in inns, hostels and taverns, usually to complement the food, just as brewpubs do today.

A craft beer or microbrewed beer generally follows the concept of the Reinheitsgebot—the Purity Order issued by the Elector of Bavaria in 1516 that established that the ingredients of Bavarian beer be limited to malt (barley or wheat), hops and water. Yeast was added later, after it was understood that it was also an "ingredient."

But the Reinheitsgebot is not a hard-and-fast rule for making distinctive beers. In England, for example, it's not uncommon for breweries to use unmalted wheat as a way of enhancing head retention. In Belgium, brewers have preserved old traditions such as using spices or fruits to flavor their distinctive ales. Both are considered classic brewing countries.

Charles Finkel, the Seattle beer importer, calls "microbrew" a West Coast term that is "more a philosophy and/or a technique than a specific size. Early on, the Association of Brewers determined that a 'microbrewery' produced fewer than 5,000 barrels of beer per year. Then several of the microbreweries exceeded the 5,000-barrel mark. Were they no longer microbreweries? Of course not. It's not a question of size, per se, but rather it's about making beer in a way that maximizes its taste while following traditional lines. That is all that a consumer wants to know."

Today, because of confusion over the term "microbrew," the industry and pundits have embraced the term "craft-brewery" and "craft-beer." These terms highlight the positive hand-crafted aspects of beers while downplaying the need for a criterion based strictly on size.

Okay, So What's a Brewpub?

We started making beer in May 1982, in a five-barrel brewery in the hallway of our building. But we couldn't actually sell our brew until we got our license on July 1.

Before we were officially in business, people were always dropping by to see how the beer was coming along, and we would give them a free taste. It didn't take very many visitors to clean us out of a five-barrel batch.

This Beer's Maybe Not for You

Introducing Grant's Ales in Yakima required a lot of the locals to traverse a steep learning curve. Head brewer Darren Waytuck recalls a story that took place on "the 23rd of December one year, when we were all enjoying a beer at the end of the day. One of the transients in the neighborhood was walking past the brewery, stuck his head in the door, pointed to the beer, and said, 'I'll have one of those!' We gave him an IPA, he took a sip, made a face, handed us back the glass, and said, 'I better get me some food.'"

Necessity is the mother of invention. Instead of locking our door, I came up with the idea of installing a few bar stools in the brewhouse entryway and creating a tiny pub, like those found in many breweries in Europe. I called the bureaucrats at the state capital of Olympia, Washington, and they said they couldn't license a brewpub because it was illegal; but they couldn't say *why* it was illegal. I couldn't find a statute that expressly outlawed a brewpub, but they continued to stonewall. Eventually, my attorney discovered that Washington State law permits a brewery to operate a maximum of one tavern.

So, Yakima became the home of the first new brewpub to be opened—not just in the state of Washington but in the entire United States—since the pre-Prohibition era. It was so small and so crowded that on a Saturday night, I'd stop by for a pint, open the door, and three people would fall out!

We drew a great cross-section of people—doctors and lawyers, farmers and factory workers. They weren't there for the ambiance; they were there for the beer. In the process, we helped change the way beer is marketed. That episode reaffirmed to me that when you hit a wall, either you go around it or push it down. The easy thing is to give up.

We were also ahead of our time in another aspect of the operation: our brewpub was probably the only tavern in the city that prohibited smoking. Some people thought I was crazy, but, once again, I didn't care. Although I occasionally enjoy a good cigar, I strongly believe that smoke keeps customers from fully appreciating the complex flavors of my beers. And that's what they should be able to do "at the source."

The Successful Brewpub

This idea of a brewpub, where you make and sell beer on the same site, was a standard method of operation in Europe, dating back to the earliest days of commercial brewing. By the late 1800s, however, the practice died off as big centralized breweries began to supply many taverns.

Today, for a brewpub to offer the best beer possible, it has to be the right size to ensure that there will be little or no old beer served. For an all-draft operation, you shouldn't serve beer that is more than three or four weeks old. For an average-sized pub in a good location, this would dictate a brew size no larger than 10 barrels. This would be very profitable at two to three brews per week and would allow production of at least five different beers, all fresh at the tap.

A brewpub has several advantages for the adventuresome, ambitious brewer, including total quality control from "mash-in" to the consumer's glass. You're in a position to receive immediate feedback—both good and bad—from the consumers.

It is estimated that 20 percent of brewpubs fail within two years of startup, mainly because of poor-quality beer, inadequate financing, over-optimistic expectations, and underestimation of the amount of skill and work involved. And don't forget the oldest rule in retail: location, location, location. That's because, when you get right down to it, a brewpub is really a kind of "theme restaurant," which succeeds or fails based on its ability to operate as such. If you don't believe me, stop by our Brewery Pub in Yakima, order the fish & chips—beer-battered with Scottish Ale, of course—and see for yourself.

We Have Beer!

After serving free beer for two months, we got our license to sell the beer on July 1, 1982, which was, by sheer coincidence, the day that a Washington State law raised the legal maximum amount of alcohol for draft beer from 3.2 percent to 8 percent by weight. (Before this change, beer over 3.2 percent could be sold only in bottles through state liquor stores.) That was fortunate for us because all of our beer is greater than 4 percent alcohol.

We started brewing two batches of beer a week. They were so popular, the kegs were drained almost as fast as they were filled. People would come to the brewery with buckets, fill them up with beer and go home.

Grant's Scottish Ale was an unabashedly premium beer, which we sold for twice what an ordinary 12-ounce draught beer would cost. It was very expensive, and it was very expensive to brew. I wasn't thinking about profit. In fact, I told the *Yakima Herald-Republic*, "Nobody's in this to make a pot of money." I've never been so prophetic.

Pouring that very first draft of Grant's Scottish Ale, and having someone actually paying for it, was one of the most satisfying moments of my life. Here I was, 54 years old and starting a new adventure. I thought about all the miles and trials, the triumphs and the disappointments, and it was a little overwhelming and emotional. And it was worth it.

The original Bert Grant's Brewery & Brewery Pub in Yakima's old opera house. We outgrew the location's limited space by the early 1990s.

Chapter Seven

BECOMING A BUSINESS

We didn't do much advertising—who had the budget for it? Anyway, I prefer letting my beer sell itself by word-of-mouth. If your beer tastes like all the others, I suppose you have to advertise to get the consumer to drink it.

We did get a lot of free publicity in the *Yakima Herald-Republic*, which wrote a Sunday feature under the headline: "Ingredients are here, world-famous hops, clear water await return of Yakima brewery." We also got favorable stories in other central Washington papers, as well as papers in Seattle and Portland, and lots of area magazines. This may seem like a small market, but it was huge for a five-barrel brewery.

In addition to my brewing duties, I was the salesman, the general manager and everything else. Unfortunately, sales were not my forte. Once a month, I'd make the 150-mile drive across the Cascade Mountains to Seattle, which was the biggest beer market in the region.

To show you how naive I was in the sales department, I didn't know back then that Seattle—thanks to Charles Finkel of Merchant du Vin—was one of the hottest markets in the country for imports, such as Bass, Guinness and Samuel Smith, which opened people's thinking to the fact that the world is not all Budweiser beer. I soon discovered that Seattle was an educated, sophisticated beer market.

ADVERTISING

Advertising can be done cleverly. In one ad that I remember for Lowenbräu, somebody says, "Let's go have beer and clams." And somebody else says, "Let's have lobster and Lowenbräu." That was a classy ad. They wouldn't do that ad today. It would be "bikini teams and Lowenbräu."

My lack of sales skills was overcome by the fact that I brewed great beer. Pretty soon, I was selling kegs to some of the best watering holes in Seattle, including F. X. McRory's, Jake O'Shaughnesseys and Blue Moon Tavern. We sold our Scottish Ale, Imperial Stout and a short-lived new brew, Light American Ale (very pale in color, with about 25 bittering units), that we introduced in October 1982.

The first year, we sold 500 barrels of ale, mainly in Seattle and Portland. The only competition we had was from Redhook, which came later. For at least a year and a half, it was just us and Redhook, then another five microbreweries popped up in Washington State alone. By that time, Redhook, owned by marketing man Paul Shipman and several well-heeled partners, unleashed an army of marketing and sales people. They swamped us, although it didn't bother me because we had only limited capacity.

Imperial Stout

Soon after we'd opened with Scottish Ale, we made our first commercial batches of Grant's Imperial Stout, a style that hadn't been seen in the U.S. for decades. It was a sipping brew, with an above-average alcohol content, designed to duplicate thick, rich, authentic British stouts that became popular around the Russian Imperial Court during the late 18th century.

Although the Russians never had much of a history of beer, these potent stouts exported from Britain really caught on. They wanted it made stronger and stronger, so there was a big competition among the English brewers to see who could make the strongest stout. To do so, the brewers added more of everything to the mash until the stout was up around 10 or 11 percent alcohol.

With Grant's Imperial Stout, in particular, I was inspired by the very full-bodied, very potent, highly hopped Guinness Foreign Extra Stout as brewed in the 1930s, 1940s and 1950s. (By contrast, today's draught Guinness is very light in body, and the roasted character comes through too strong for my taste. In the old days, they used a lot more black malt and caramel malt to fill out the body.)

GUINNESS

Guinness today is a far cry from the family operation it was when I first started going there in the 1950s—when I knew the operating manager quite well, actually. The family is still involved with the brewery as shareholders, but doesn't have much say. As happens with many family businesses that grow, they left the running of the brewery to management people who, over the years, lost sight of what the company stood for. Guinness beer is now a pale imitation of what it was 40 years ago. Guinness now uses less malt and caramel malt, but about the same burnt barley that has always been the dominant flavor in Guinness, anyway. There has been a more subtle difference in the draft beer's body. The draft beer we now get in the States is very thin—only around 4.2 percent alcohol by volume.

At the time, nobody else in America (and maybe even the world) was making a stout like mine. England's Courage brewery made one batch of Imperial Stout every few years—very expensive and narrowly distributed. You'd have to search all over London to find a bottle. I didn't like the Courage stout as much as the really old Guinness. And those Guinness stouts were made only for such special occasions as the Royal Wedding.

The old emigrant British brewmasters that I worked with in Ontario made a lighter, Canadian-style stout that was more malty than the English style.

By contrast, I feel that stout should be heavy in body and "mouth-feel," and have a lot of flavor impact. Some Guinness stouts that I analyzed back in the '40s and early '50s were reaching as much as 100 bitterness units. (By contrast, today's Budweiser checks in around 10.) We started out our Imperial Stout at about 90-100 bitterness units—but it was very hard to reach a value that high on a consistent basis because it's close to the solubility limit of the bittering compounds in hops. We brought the bittering down to 75 or 80 units, which is still quite bitter (but not overpowering, because of the rich maltiness of the beer).

Most imperial stouts made today are 9 to 11 percent alcohol by volume. But when we reintroduced the style to America in 1982, our target of around 6 to 7 percent was huge. In fact, because there's so much fermentable sugar in the wort for Grant's Imperial Stout, we have to ferment it at a lower temperature than our other beers. Otherwise, it goes so fast that it will blow the safety valve and come out of the tank!

Obviously, Imperial Stout was a tougher sell for us than Scottish Ale. But the first few pubs that carried it were extremely loyal, and they eventually developed a faithful clientele. Your palate has to get used to this kind of beer. I certainly wouldn't start someone who is used to standard American lager on Imperial Stout, which is an entirely different experience.

It's got lots of character, thanks to the caramel malt and black malt, and the hops, of course, for bitterness. We also add honey to the brewkettle, as a way of imparting a smoothness and "roundness" of body with a hint of flavor. As with other stouts, you boil the hops a long time to bring up the bitterness and blow off the hop aroma. What you get with Grant's Imperial Stout is the aroma of the chocolate malt and the burnt malt.

We intended it as a seasonal product, but it became so popular that we made it a year-round brew. In 1984, Grant's Imperial Stout was awarded First Place in the consumer preference poll at the annual National Great American Beer Festival in Colorado. Oh, by the way, Grant's Scottish Ale took second place. This was back in the days when consumers voted, before some brewers started "buying" votes with promotional give-aways. (We learned a painful marketing lesson over the next few years: it's hard for great beer alone to compete for consumers' favor against free T-shirts, buttons and pint glasses. Looking back, I suppose we should have put an item in our annual budget for "temporary tattoos.")

I like to drink Imperial Stout with a good steak, or as a dessert beer with Viennese-style chocolate cake or a good strong Sacher torte. I love the combination of the sweetness of the chocolate cake and the bitterness of the Imperial Stout, with both of them having that very rich chocolate character to them.

I remember back in those early days, we would spend all day brewing, and then all night loading trucks. When we finally finished at about six in the morning, as everyone else in town was having their morning coffee, we were breakfasting on Imperial Stout.

AWARD-WINNING IMPERIAL STOUT

In 1998, judges at the 1998 Brewing Industry International Awards (held in Burton-on-Trent, England) nominated our Imperial Stout for one of the competition's top prizes. It was nice to see that the judges had such great taste.

The competition's judges, an international collection of professional brewers, evaluated more than 800 beers produced by 200 breweries in 32 countries. Beers were sampled in 20 separate categories based on type, style, and packaging (bottles, cans or draft). Our Imperial Stout was nominated for the Grand Prize in the "Dark Milds, Stouts & Porters (packaged)" category reserved for heartier brews.

Oh, My Aching Head!

In 1983, in the midst of all this great fun we were having with Grant's Ales, something happened to me that almost ended the party—permanently. One afternoon, while doing my business at the brewery, I suddenly was struck by the most blinding, horrendous headache you can imagine. It felt like someone had slugged me over the head with a pickax. Bang! I just about collapsed. I got into my chair, and I sat down and said to myself, "Something's wrong."

I made it over to my doctor's, and he immediately put me in the hospital, where I was given a CAT scan. They found a brain tumor, and took it out, cutting away a big part of my olfactory nerves. The first person at my bedside when I woke up was a friend of mine who is a radiologist. He said, "You're very lucky, Bert. Ten years ago, we found all of these tumors on post-mortems. *All.*"

I was out of commission for about a month. Luckily, I had already taught my assistant Dan Boutillier my secrets of tasting and smelling beer, so we were able to carry on pretty much business as usual.

What effect did the operation have on me? I had to learn a different way to taste. I can still sense a lot of the flavor of beer, but the more subtle tastes and smells, especially in the hops, escape me now. Some say that's why my beers are "over-the-top" hoppy—I add hops to the level where I can smell them!

India Pale Ale

In 1983, we reintroduced India Pale Ale to the American market. The only other beer in the U.S. that carried the name "IPA" was one produced by Ballantine Beer—and by the early 1980s, it had become a weak interpretation of the style (despite having been glorious in its heyday during the 1960s and earlier).

MICHAEL JACKSON ON GRANT'S IPA

Michael Jackson, the internationally famous beer writer, credits Bert Grant with being the first American microbrewer to reintroduce IPA as a "pale, assertive, intensely dry, bitter aromatic style of beer". . . that has "been widely copied and has become a new American style.

"The combination of pale color, aromatic hop character and an intensity of bitterness far exceeded any IPA made in Britain. Even some of the British brewers have been inspired by that in recent years. They are not making such intensely bitter examples, but they have clearly been influenced by that style."

When he first tasted Grant's IPA, "I was just stunned by the bitterness of it. I just loved the bitterness of it," Jackson recalled. "I thought, 'Christ, he's really going to do this. Bert really expects people to buy this?'

"It was like hearing Charlie Parker for the first time, and wondering, 'Are people really going to buy these records?' I have sampled Grant's IPA many times since, and always found it very hoppy. But nothing could match the shock of that first encounter."

India Pale Ale was a type of beer developed by British breweries for shipment to troops stationed at the far reaches of the Empire back in the 1800s. These beers were brewed with high hop rates and high original gravities (fermentable sugars). They finished fermentation in big wooden casks during their long ship journey, arriving at their destination in peak condition. One of the more popular destinations was India, hence the development of beers known as India Pale Ale, or IPA.

The English brewers knew that using more hops improved the stability of their beers. (We know today that, while hops don't kill bacteria, the iso-humulones in the hops keep bacteria from reproducing.) So, they doubled the hop rate for IPAs and did a little extra boiling. They tried to make very pale beers, but could get only a copper color due to the quality of their barley malt (a result of poor temperature control during the malting process).

I believe my India Pale Ale is one of the few "properly hopped" beers in America, with a hop rate around 50 bitterness units. The hops dominate because the IPA is made exclusively with pale malt. Although there's a lot of hop flavor, it doesn't bite your tongue. Well, OK, maybe it does a little.

ROGER PROTZ ON GRANT'S IPA

"Bert's influence can be seen in the fact that a few years ago the British Guild of Beer Writers held a seminar in Britain on India Pale Ale. They had British-brewed IPAs especially for the occasion. Several American brewers came over with IPAs, and theirs were truer to the style than most of the British ones. A lot of the IPAs in Britain are just caricatures of the style.

"That inspiration comes from Bert. The fact that people are re-creating IPAs with the right sort of strength of about 6 or 7 percent of alcohol by volume, and a very intense hoppiness, says a lot for the pioneering work he has done."

My goal for IPA was a clean, sharp beer, with a reasonable balance of malt to support—but not overpower—the hoppiness. When you pour it, you notice the beautiful creamy head; the more hops, it turns out, the better the head. In India Pale Ale, we use Galena hops for bitterness and Cascade, added near the end of the brewing process, for aroma. Grant's IPA actually was one of the first really pale ales made in the western U.S. to feature Cascades.

Analytically, Scottish Ale and India Pale Ale are close to being the same bitterness level. But the Scottish Ale uses only Cascade hops, while the IPA primarily uses Galena hops. There is a definite flavor difference between the two as far as bitterness is concerned, and a huge difference in terms of aroma. With the Cascade, you get a lovely citrusy-floral character; Galena gives you an incredibly "clean," straightforward bitterness with just a trace of hoppy resinous flavor. It's a different ballgame. That's why we add a dose of Cascades to the IPA toward the end of the boil, to provide some of those citrus-floral notes.

I like to drink IPA with Thai food, and some of the combinations of ginger and pepper that are used in Korean foods. That bitterness sort of negates the effect of the hot pepper; it cleans your palate.

Since the introduction of Grant's IPA in 1983, the Pacific Northwest has become quite a region for IPA, boasting examples that are assertively hoppy, with good flavor and a robust finish. It's nice to see the style make such a vibrant comeback—it reminds me of watching my children grow up.

Yakima Herald-Republic photo

All smiles because I get to work here every day:
the new Bert Grant's Brewery,
which we built using Europe's classic
"brew tower" model.

Chapter Eight

LET'S GO A MILLION DOLLARS IN DEBT

In the mid-1980s, our beers continued to sell well, particularly in Seattle and Portland. But we had a hard time finding a distributor that was more interested in quality than quantity. In hindsight, we should have bypassed the major distributors and hired our own salesman based in Seattle, but we couldn't afford it.

Even though we were grossing about $400,000 on sales of 3,500 barrels by 1985, money was always a problem. I tried to borrow money from banks, but they looked at our cash flow and laughed.

We operated on a shoestring, always waiting for the next check from the distributor to make the payroll for our staff of 10—one person running the office, three in the brewery, two in the pub and three part-timers (later) helping with bottling. Jana Johnson became manager of the pub. She really enhanced its success by increasing the menu and the hours, and bringing in musicians. I didn't draw a salary. I continued to work full-time as Steiner's technical director, and put my wages into the brewery so that we could keep running.

Despite our problems, Yakima Brewing & Malting was featured in *Money* magazine's "Money Makers" section. Ironic. Let that serve as a reminder: don't always believe what you read in the media.

THE BEER COMES FIRST

Dan Boutillier joined Grant's in December 1982, and is currently production manager. Darren Waytuck came aboard in April 1984, and is now the head brewer. They both remember the first absolute that Bert told them when they were hired: "No matter what you do here, always remember: The beer comes first."

THE LOAN ARRANGER

At the end of 1986, faced with a flat market for draught beer, we invested $150,000 in a new bottling operation, which would enable us to expand our distribution to stores and supermarkets. It was a tight squeeze to fit the bottling equipment in the old opera house.

Again, my decision wasn't based on any market surveys. I don't believe in them, and they usually cost you your first year's profit—if you have any. Although I was initially against bottling the beer, I eventually changed my mind because, over the years, a lot of people had asked us for bottled beer. That's why we chose to do it, pure and simple.

The only problem was that we weren't set up for such an operation. When we started bottling, we had to store new bottles in the parking lot, haul them in when we needed to bottle the beer, and then store all the full bottles out in the parking lot until we were finished. (At that point, we couldn't afford a cold room big enough to hold bottled beer.) Then we filled up our bottle shop with the full goods.

When I thought I could afford to, I went half-time with Steiner and worked on expanding our production. To meet rising demand, we replaced the 5-barrel brewkettle with a 10-barrel kettle, and added more fermenters until there was no space to grow within the old opera house.

RUMORS

The beer market is so full of rumors. Back in the late '80s, we had some overaged draft beer that the distributor had tucked away in the back of the warehouse for about three months and forgotten about. You can't store unpasteurized draft beer that long. So, all kinds of rumors went through the town: "Bert Grant's beer has turned bad!" It was six kegs to six accounts, and word spread like wildfire, even though the keg before and the keg afterward were fine. It took a helluva long time to push that down.

When we changed distributors in Seattle and other markets during the mid-1990s, some competitors told customers that I had died and the brewery was closed. They didn't say that we had changed distributors.

In order to keep growing, we needed to invest in expansion of the brewery. In 1990, I applied for a $900,000 Small Business Administration loan, which had to be backed up by a personal guarantee. I approached the other investors in the brewery, but no one wanted to be a signatory. So, I saw that I had to be the one to step forward. Believe me, I had to do a lot of talking to convince my Yakima banker that a guy whose main asset was shares in the brewery would be good for a $900,000 loan. But the quality of our beer saved the day! The banker knew that the beer was good, and the pub was busy every time he stopped by. So, he backed us, and the SBA went along with it.

My helpful son-in-law Mauro Berretta, the husband of my daughter Shannon, helped to come up with additional money. Any positive cash flow was pumped back into the brewery in the form of new equipment.

A New Brewery

We couldn't come to a satisfactory agreement with our landlord, so we needed to look elsewhere. We selected a one-and-a-half-acre property adjacent to S. S. Steiner, where we built a 20,000-square-foot brewery.

I designed the brewhouse, which features a larger all-copper, direct-fire kettle, new stainless-steel "unitank" fermenters, and an old-fashioned 40-foot brew tower, which utilizes gravity to move ingredients between the various stages of brewing.

The earliest commercial breweries were all "gravity fed." (In the old days, when you approached a town, the first thing you could see was a church steeple and the second was the local brewery's tower.) We use the same gravity-fed process because it is superior—in terms of its effect on the beer—to the pumps frequently used in other breweries. First of all, if you pump the mash into the lauter tun, you break up the grain husks, which slows down your run off the wort, and imparts some grainier flavors to the beer. Second, and more important, if you pump the wort out of the brewkettle—where you've just gone to all the trouble to precipitate proteins out of the liquid—you break up the protein "chains" again as the wort moves into the fermenter. That can make for hazy beer.

So, overall, the brew tower not only saves energy but also adds to the quality of our beers.

The new brewery went into operation in September 1991, and essentially doubled our production to about 12,000 barrels in the first year. By that time, our line included Scottish Ale, Imperial Stout, IPA, Celtic Ale, Weis Beer and Spiced Ale (for winter), which we sold in 10 states and the District of Columbia.

Around the same time, it had become obvious that the pub was too small—it seated only about 35 people. So, we leased space in much larger quarters in the north end of Yakima's restored train depot—just across the street from the opera house—which was a better location and could seat as many as 250 people. The "new" Brewery Pub opened in January 1990. Paneled with oak and lighted by stained glass windows of my own creation, the pub has the intimate feel of a neighborhood gathering spot. Our manager, Jana Johnson, eventually was able to book into the pub a lot of great musicians, some with national reputations, such as legendary trumpet player Maynard Ferguson and his band, and the folksinger Jesse Colin Young.

We began featuring pub-style food for lunch and dinner seven days a week, such as a ploughman's lunch, British Banger, Scotch eggs, Cornish pasties, Scottish meat pie, a couple of German dishes I happen to like and, of course, fish and chips, as well as a full selection of Grant's Ales. And there's still no smoking, because I don't want smoke to interfere with people tasting my beers "at the source"—and it's my pub.

Microbrewing in the Pacific Northwest

According to Charles Finkel, founder of beer importer Merchant du Vin and the Pike Brewing Company, the Pacific Northwest has always been a hotbed of serious beer drinkers who had been frustrated by the beer that was available commercially. Many of them became home brewers because "they knew damn well that they could make much better beer themselves than they could buy. The region has always been a little counterculture. The people who come to the Northwest are very independent in mind, and not interested in emulating Eastern cities. We don't have the old traditions of other regions. You start out with a clean slate, with no prejudice to existing tastes. So, we set trends with beer, wine, food and coffee.

"Before the onset of the Northwest microbrewery phenomena, most people were not used to drinking beer with any hops at all. Even few serious writers about beer were exposed to beer hopped over 25 bitterness units. So, here comes this hop head, Bert Grant, and he's hopping his brews to 60 or more bitterness units; no wonder people were taken aback."

Also, in 1990, I was presented with the Industry Recognition Award at the National Micro-Brewery Conference in Denver. The award recognizes an individual most responsible for "contributing to the growth of the beer industry through education, research or the dissemination of information." What a wonderful honor. It makes me feel good, knowing that other people have recognized that my efforts in this business have made a difference.

CROSBY, STILLS & NASH

I knew that our beer was achieving more than cult status a few years ago, when I was in Denver. I wanted to try the beer in one of their new brew-pubs. I walked in the front door with my wife, and about 20 people who were sitting around a big table got on their feet and started applauding. I looked behind me to see who the clapping was for. It was for me. They recognized me from my picture on the labels of my beer.

One of them invited us to the table, and he introduced me to the group as "the father of all the microbrews." He was the manager for Crosby, Stills and Nash, who were playing Denver that evening. One thing led to another, and that night my wife and I went out to the show at Red Rocks, where we got to stand on stage behind the speakers.

They invited us to the following month's show at the outdoor Gorge Amphitheater (overlooking the Columbia River) in Washington State. We loaded a few cases of beer in the trunk and again sat on the stage and enjoyed another wonderful performance. We had dinner with them that night. They were a good group.

Sampling my favorite Scottish Ale at our 15th Anniversary in 1997: bureaucratic entanglements can't hold back the success of great beer.

Chapter Nine

MY "FOOD FIGHT" WITH THE ATF

I remember when vitamin B-12 was discovered in beer, back in the late 1940s. At the time, I was at Canadian Breweries' lab, and the more we analyzed beers, the more B vitamins we found—B-5, B-6, B-12. They come from the yeast and by-products of yeast fermentation. We also discovered that all-malt beers can provide a notable amount of protein in addition to "just calories."

In 1992, the Siebel Institute in Chicago, which offers laboratory services to breweries across North America, performed a comprehensive analysis of our Scottish Ale. At around the same time, the federal government announced new food-labeling rules that would make it easier for consumers to evaluate the nutritional value of the products they were buying. So, we decided to follow the food guidelines by printing information showing the results of Siebel's analysis. Far from offering "empty calories," it turns out, a 12-ounce bottle of Grant's Scottish Ale contains 145 calories, no fat or cholesterol, 2.24 grams of protein and 12.7

grams of carbohydrates; and each bottle provides 4 percent of the U.S. Recommended Daily Allowance of protein, as well as 4.6 percent of vitamin B-2, 14.6 percent of niacin, 62.5 percent of folacin and 170 percent of B-12.

Although the data indicates that a bottle of Grant's Scottish couldn't possibly qualify as a complete "meal," one or two bottles a day theoretically could make a contribution to an adult diet. We used to joke that you wouldn't starve to death drinking Grant's!

Federal regulations prohibit nutritional labels on bottles of beer, so we decided to print up the analysis data on Scottish Ale six-packs, as well as T-shirts and some in-store display materials. But then one day, an agent from the Bureau of Alcohol, Tobacco and Firearms (ATF) walked into the brewery and ordered us to stop using the nutritional information because it violated federal law. The specific law was a 1950s-era regulation on beer advertising—not just beer labeling—that prohibited any statement "that the use of any malt beverage has curative or therapeutic effects if such statement is untrue in any particular or tends to create a misleading impression." According to the ATF, the six-packs and other materials qualified as "advertising," and therefore were violating the law.

In other words, by reprinting a scientific nutritional analysis (including protein and vitamin content), I was deceiving people into thinking that my Scottish Ale would benefit their health. To me, this seemed nuts. After all, it's the same nutritional information that the government *requires* on the likes of Twinkies and "Chunky Monkey" ice cream. One option, we were told, was that we could remove all the vitamin content and list only the calorie, fat, protein and carbohydrate content. But we still would have had to destroy all the packaging and advertising material that we had developed. Thankfully, after some negotiation, the ATF agreed to let us use up all the existing materials.

The whole episode got lots of exposure in the national media. *The Wall Street Journal*, for example, pointed out that a bottle of Grant's Scottish "had slightly more protein than a dry bowl of cornflakes, with half the carbohydrates, twice the potassium, much less sodium, no fat and a stellar dose of B-vitamins." Several other publications wrote similar stories, and I was eager to speak out. But my friends in the beer industry warned me to "shut up and don't get the ATF mad!"

Cider House Rules

A few months later, in April 1993, the ATF came visiting again. They ordered me to stop production of Grant's Yakima Cider—a hard cider like those popular in England and catching on today in America—because they classified it as wine, and therefore it was taxable at a different, higher rate than beer. Actually, because it was carbonated, it probably qualified as a "sparkling wine" like Champagne and would have been taxable at an even higher rate!

Federal law, it turns out, stipulated that a hard cider had to be made from "apple juice only" to take advantage of an exemption (intended for roadside farm-cider stands) from the wine tax. Because ours was made with apple juice *concentrate*, we were told, it was taxable as a wine. Of course, to make concentrate, you take water out of pure juice. To make our cider, we remixed the concentrate with pure water—basically reconstituting it—so I argued that it wasn't any different than using apple juice to begin with. But the ATF didn't buy it.

That meant that we had to become a certified wine producer if we wanted to continue making the cider; our brewery license wasn't enough. In addition, based on the cider we'd produced up to that time, the ATF said we owed a $1.07 per gallon wine tax, interest on the taxes, and penalties that could exceed $70,000. Fortunately, after the media caught wind of the story again, we managed to reach an agreement with the ATF to pay only a portion of the taxes.

We had produced 65,000 gallons of the cider by April 1993. At the time, it represented about 5 percent of our $1.8 million in sales. Rather than continue to fight the regulations, we begrudgingly created a replacement: Grant's Apple Honey Ale. This product met the basic ATF rules for qualifying as a beer, not a wine. It was about 40 percent malt-based, with an extremely minimal hop rate; the rest was just the same as our cider had been, except for the addition of honey to round out the flavor. Apple Honey was a good product, even if it was not particularly profitable to make (mainly because of the cost of the honey). Still, after some positive initial consumer response, sales slowed down well below the level of the cider. It got to the point where I was finding a lot of "aging" Apple Honey in markets that I visited. I didn't want that to affect our overall quality standard, so we eventually dropped it from the line.

Waiter, There's Some Fruit in My Beer!

Apple Honey Ale aside, I frequently get asked for my opinion of fruit-flavored beers. Now, I like eating an apricot—which is a good thing when you live in Yakima, the heart of Washington's fruit-growing country—and you know I like having a beer, but I don't particularly like apricot beer. Or blueberry beer. Or cherry beer. Or mango ale. The only fruit flavor that works in beer is cranberry, but you have to have the right balance. Just a bit of cranberry juice, particularly in a pale beer, gives you a nice purple color, and a nice drying effect on the beer.

The year-round range of Grant's Ales in 1998:
I like this "family portrait"
almost as much as the one on page 16!

Chapter Ten

ROUNDING OUT THE LINE

In the 1990s, we continued to add a variety of new beers to our assortment. Like my original ales, all are naturally carbonated during fermentation. If you don't ferment under pressure in this way, you lose all the aromatic compounds that the yeast produce. Many big brewers allow CO2 to vent off during fermentation, then they "force carbonate" the beer to a relatively high "fizzy" level right before bottling or kegging. This improves shelf-life, but it doesn't do much for taste. Even the big brewers that capture CO2 from fermentation then purify it, taking out the aromatics, before putting it back in their beer.

Grape Versus Grain

I've always believed that a major difference between making wine and making beer is this: If you give the same grapes to a half-dozen vintners there will be a very strong family resemblance to each of their wines. If you have good grapes, there is not much a vintner can do wrong, but there is nothing any of them can do if they have bad grapes.

With beer, if you give the same malt and the same hops to a half-dozen brewmasters, you will get six different beers. And even if you have problems with the malt and hops, there are a lot of things a brewmaster can do to make good beer. If you have a hop with a very bad aroma, for example, you just boil it for a long time, and the unwanted aromatics will disappear. If you have a malt with very low enzymes, you just leave it in the mash cooker for a longer time.

Perfect Porter

Porter was a style of dark ale introduced in the 18th century by large British breweries, which made their own very dark porter malt. Because the malt was comparatively cheap to make in quantity, the breweries could make large quantities of the beer and sell it cheaply. The style, whose rise coincided with the Industrial Revolution, became a favorite of manual laborers, including many working London porters, who gave the beer its name.

Porter has a lower alcohol content than stout—in fact, the name "stout" refers to the fact that the style originally was a form of "stout" (strong) porter. I think porter should have much less black malt or black barley flavor than stout, and place a little more emphasis on the hop aroma.

I first learned about porter from the Scottish brewmasters that I trained under when I worked at Canadian Breweries. When I first went to work for the brewery in 1945, those guys were already in their 60s, so their knowledge of porters dated back to the pre-World War I era. They assured me that—in their opinion—there wasn't a porter in North America that was being brewed the way it should. (Actually, there weren't many porters brewed in North America.)

Most of the porters produced in Canada and all of the porters produced in the U.S. were made by adding caramel color to a lager or an ale after fermentation. The brewery supply companies sold a sweet reddish-brown product called "porterine"—a burnt sugar produced by roasting ordinary sucrose. We made a couple of porters in Toronto that were acceptable, but they weren't proper porters.

Brewing my porter is complicated by the fact that we use so many different malts: pale malt, caramel malt, chocolate malt, black malt, as well as peat-smoked malt (our only imported ingredient, from Britain). The peat-smoked malt—the same kind of malt that's used to make Scotch whiskey—is included to give a hint of the smokiness that surely was present in the original English porters, which were developed at a time when all malt was dried over smoky direct fires. To provide a little bit of the vanilla character you might have gotten from oak casks, we originally aged the porter with wood chips for a day or two. You might still detect a hint of vanilla in it today.

We call it Perfect Porter because it's a balancing of all those different kinds of malts, plus the suggestion of oak or vanilla. One day, back when we were developing it, we had done five or six trial brews. On the sixth batch, all the right tastes came together. Most porters taste like coffee; ours tasted like chocolate. Everyone who tried it said, "This is perfect." The name stuck, and so did the beer.

In his book *Beer: A User's Guide,* Michael Jackson writes: "[Grant's] brand name Perfect Porter is hardly modest, but the alcohol content (4 percent) is; despite which, this beer is astonishingly well rounded. In both body and flavor, with suggestions of cocoa powder, toasted nuts, and a touch of peat."

It's a sipping beer. When you taste it, I want it to be very complicated and have different flavors all the way down. You take a mouthful. It goes down your throat slowly and smoothly. The back of your palate gets the effect of the black malt. After a while, you get the smoky character. You taste the caramel, you taste the chocolate, you taste the vanilla, all these things; not necessarily sequentially, but you can pick them all out. A flavor symphony.

I like to drink Porter with spicy, strong-flavored dishes or a well-browned beef stew because it enhances your palate. It's great with fine cigars because of smoky synergy with the peat-smoked malt.

HefeWeizen

We originally produced a filtered wheat ale, called Grant's Weis ("white") Beer, that was clear, clean, sharp and refreshing. (Despite the name, it was not a Berliner-style weisse.) But Widmer Brewing of Portland, Oregon, then came out with a mild-tasting, unfiltered, cloudy hefeweizen (German for "yeast/wheat") with a distinctive yeasty taste, which soon became the definitive Northwest version of the wheat beer style. Soon after, other breweries such as Pyramid, Redhook and Nor'Wester followed suit with their own cloudy wheat beers. Our clear Weis Beer took a beating in the market.

We wanted to provide consumers with a good starter beer, so we reformulated the Weis Beer and reintroduced it as Grant's HefeWeizen. The cloudiness comes from a second, Bavarian yeast strain that we add after primary fermentation.

Most American hefeweizens are sweet, malty and mild. Grant's has a distinctive, clean, dry flavor that comes primarily from the wheat malt (we use about 30 percent wheat malt) and the secondary yeast (which remains in the bottle or keg). We also add an above-average dose of Cascade hops to give it more flavor and aroma.

Observing an old German tradition, most American pubs or restaurants serve hefeweizen with a slice of lemon. That's fine for improving the flavor of some of the very mild American-style versions, but you don't need a lemon or lime when you drink Grant's HefeWeizen. My beer's got enough flavor from the wheat malt and above-average hopping. Besides, I'm seeing a lot of HefeWeizen drinkers these days who have joined the "NFL" team—the first word is "No," the last is "Lemon," and you can figure out the one in the middle!

HefeWeizen is one of the few beers that I like tasting cold. If I were setting up a beer tasting, I would start with HefeWeizen served with a mild soup or a salad course. I also drink it with lighter food, such as fish, chicken and chowders.

Amber Ale

After Scottish Ale, Imperial Stout and IPA—not to mention the short-lived, draft-only Light American Ale and Light Stout (which we really should have called a porter)—the next brew we introduced was Celtic Ale. Michael Jackson described it as "less obviously malty than roasty and hoppy, and very dark. Like several of Grant's brews, it is a law unto itself."

Unfortunately, as had happened earlier with Apple Honey Ale, sales of Celtic were slow. That meant that a lot of beer was "aging" on store shelves, which was no good for the beer, or for consumers who ultimately bought it. Faced with this quality issue, and the fact that so many of our competitors were introducing amber ales, we made a decision to discontinue the Celtic Ale and replace it with Grant's Amber Ale. We want to cover a vast spectrum of beer categories, so that consumers have a choice of a distinctive Grant's beer in each category.

Grant's Amber Ale is a full-bodied and smooth beer, more user-friendly than our Scottish Ale. In general, Amber Ale is more malty and a lot less hoppy than the Scottish, but it still has enough hops to notice. With a bitterness unit level of about 25, the aromatic Mt. Hood and Tettnang hops (both German "aroma" hops) balance the sweetness you'd find in most other amber ales and provide an enticing character that's more spicy than floral. The most important thing we do is increase the caramel malt profile in the Amber. This supports what I like to call "the big mouthful of malt" with a noticeable butterscotch character. I like to drink Amber Ale at lunch with burgers or pizza.

Has Anyone Invented a New Category of Beer?

Not really—only variations on existing categories. For example, light beer just uses enzymes after the mash to get all the carbohydrates converted to fermentable sugar. That makes it a very dry, higher-alcohol product (which, of course, is watered down to normal levels prior to release).

Dry beer is not a valid category because it was never really defined. Dry beer was just a kind of light beer, in some cases, a light beer with more alcohol in which all the sugars had been fermented out (leaving it "dry" as opposed to sweet).

Things like "extra cold filtered" and "ice beer" are marketing gimmicks. Everybody filters their beer cold; nobody filters their beer warm. Up in Canada in the '80s, they allowed brewers to remove some of the ice, which is another way to increase the alcohol content. I suppose you could look at things like American-style wheat beers and maybe hoppy, pale "West Coast" ales as new styles—but even these really are just modern twists on other types of beers.

Seasonal Ales

In 1997, we introduced a line of four seasonal ales designed to showcase individual varieties of Yakima Valley hops. Each beer is meant to highlight the character of a single, specific hop variety—not just bitterness, not just aroma, but the overall impressions you get from that type of hop. Different hops, after all, have different characters just like wine grapes: Cascades may be citrusy and floral, while Fuggles are kind of herbal and earthy.

The one I like best is Fresh Hop Ale, which we make with the first hops of each year's harvest. My friends in the wine business call it a "beer-jolais nouveau." We take green hop blossoms right off the ripe hop vines—before they are dried and processed—and rush them to the brewery. (You've got only an hour or two to use the cones before they start to wilt.) The name of the game is not to get the bitterness but to bring out the volatile, fleeting high note that you get from fresh hops, which we add right at the end of the boil.

Our Winter Ale is a complex malt-based brew that uses spicy, herbal Mt. Hood hops (which are a relative of Germany's Hallertau hop). Most brewers make winter beers with English-style hops, but I've never been afraid to break the mold. SpringFest Ale uses a zesty Northwest version of English "Fuggle" hops, called Willamettes, that accents the beer's deep amber maltiness. Summer Ale features the distinctive aroma of Chinook hops, which give it a citrus-like taste that some describe as lemony. As a matter of fact, our first edition of Summer Ale was dry-hopped—a process in which you let new hops steep in the maturing beer, imparting their aroma and flavor (but not overt bitterness) to the finished brew. It went over so well that we're going to introduce a version year-round called Glorious Golden Ale. All still without any kind of marketing surveys, I'm proud to say!

Freshness

Freshness, of course, is crucial to the ultimate enjoyment of the beer. For our unpasteurized draft beer, we ideally like to see it consumed from the keg within no more than six weeks—provided that you keep it cold. Keg beer, with a minimum of head space and low oxygen levels in the head space, can be transported and bumped around on a refrigerated truck without too much damage. But if you had unpasteurized keg beer on a warm truck for a whole warm afternoon, it would be gone. It wouldn't taste right.

In the old days, to some degree, beers were protected from the effects of heat and transport by being stronger in flavor and alcohol content. If you had an all-malt draft beer with two or three times the hops of beers today, you could bounce the draft around on the truck for the whole day, bring it back, serve it, and you'd still think it was good beer. Today, even when you bounce around beer from the major breweries on a truck for a whole day, it changes the flavor of the beer for the worse, because you have very little hops and malt to protect it from oxidation.

By comparison, I've tasted bottles of our Imperial Stout that have sat on a shelf for two years, and it's still a very good stout. You could tell it was different, but you wouldn't say it was bad.

ALCOHOL CONTENT

Almost every large brewery is producing high-alcohol beer, and then diluting it down to the proper alcohol level before bottling.

It's done for economic reasons. Instead of making beer at 12 degrees Plato (a measure of fermentable material in the wort), they'll make it at 16 or 17 Plato, and then just before bottling, they add 25 to 30 percent water, to bring it down to the equivalent finished alcohol content of a 12 degree Plato beer. That way, you get 25 to 30 percent more beer out of the same equipment.

The big breweries have been doing this for a while. We were at Coors a few years ago, and we were going through the final filtration room, which had 20-foot-long filter pads.

The Coors guy said, "Would you like to taste some beer?"

He opened the spigot on top of the filter and poured it down.

I thought, "This is better than any Coors I ever had." Of course, that was before they put the water in.

This has been going on since the '50s. Part of the reason has to do with taxes—state and federal. You're taxed on how much alcohol is in the final product—the bottle or keg—not the amount of alcohol you use in the process.

When we ship draft beer around the country, we demand that it be kept refrigerated. I've had our draft in Atlanta, and it's just as good as if it were in Seattle. This is particularly true of our Scottish Ale. I don't care if our beer travels in a refrigerated truck 25 miles or 250 miles, just as long as we adhere to our standards.

I almost always can tell the difference between a Grant's bottle tasted right off the bottling line and a bottle bought later in a grocery store. (That's the best part about founding a brewery:

you always can get brewery-fresh beer!) Because I like to see what the consumer is getting, I take some of our beers home and let them sit for four months to see if they're OK.

We also keep lab samples at the brewery for regular analysis. We find that the hops do not change a lot in flavor; the bitterness stays about the same. You can detect some oxidation in the aroma, but usually after four months it's not that noticeable. Beer that has been stored at room temperature will noticeably change, but if it's kept cold, I can't tell much of a difference.

I would love to figure out how to get "cask-conditioned" flavor in a bottled beer that would keep for at least a month. I can do it for a while, but it doesn't last more than a week.

What's Next? It's in the Pilot Brewing Room

Someone once asked me how many ideas I haven't tried yet. About 6,845 to be precise! So many beers and so little time.

One of my ideas is to try to make a totally different, strong ale (6 percent or higher) that would be about the color and maltiness of the Amber Ale, but with a bit of smoked malt and a lot of hops. What I have in mind are Nugget hops, which contribute a distinctive aroma and a very sharp bitterness, kind of like the Galenas in Grant's India Pale Ale. I'm trying to find the right balance between the bitterness and the aroma.

Our pilot brewery is my hobby shop. It looks like a wall-mounted maze of tubes. There's nothing high-tech or expensive about this operation—everything is made out of parts from the local hardware store. We've got a five-gallon stainless steel pot, two five-gallon copper kettles (someone always jokes about bringing over a lobster), a "Little Chief" two-burner gas camp-stove (which is powered by a five-gallon tank of propane gas), and a crude but efficient cooling system. The science of the process is our ability to precisely measure the weight of ingredients, the volume of liquids, the temperature and the brewing time.

Although the pilot brewing room doesn't have much in the way of scientific equipment, it's right next to the lab, where we do a lot of experimentation on ingredients. For example, we may have been using the same yeast in the plant for six months, but we often vary the amount of yeast we use, depending on its condition. Consistency in brewing is very important.

As a home brewer for four decades, I believe the most important thing is to follow certain basic rules and use the right ingredients. After that, it's a matter of technique. In this next chapter, I want to offer the home brewer some helpful hints to make great beer.

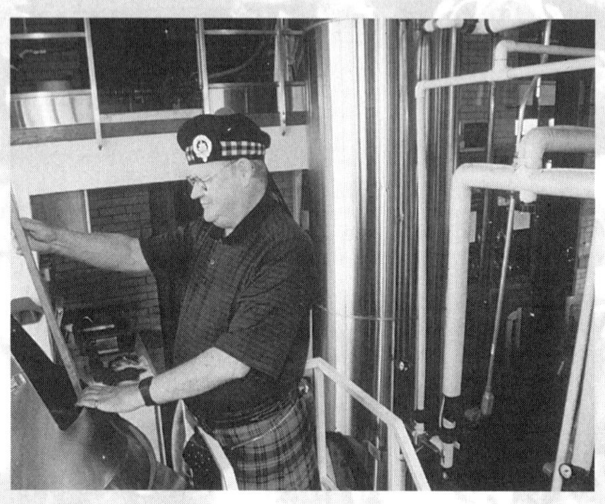

The Brewery Pub's five-barrel system (which includes our original copper kettle) provides a grander scale for experimentation than I had in my basement home-brew days.

Chapter Eleven

HINTS FOR HOME BREWING

When it comes to home brewing, I have certain core beliefs. First of all, if you're not going to use all grain, I recommend using only malt syrups. Corn syrup gives you a sweetness at the end of fermentation that you just can't get rid of in the flavor of the beer.

Yeast—liquid not dried—should be purchased from a home brew shop with a good reputation, with a proprietor who knows his stuff. Look for a big, reliable commercial company such as Wyeast from Mt. Hood, Oregon. Don't use Fleischmann's, because it's meant for baking, not for beer! Start cultivating your yeast at least one day before in sterile facilities.

Yeast is related to fungi. If you let the yeast grow long enough under the wrong conditions, it will develop filaments, just as fungus does, and different strains will do different things. Because yeast is quite changeable, it's very important to keep the conditions the same every time you make a brew, so you maintain a consistency in the flavor of the beer.

I recommend that home brewers use direct gas fire—whether propane or natural gas—because cooking temperature is easier to control with a gas fire than an electric burner. A big, heavy-gauge 10-gallon aluminum kitchen pot with a direct gas fire is fine for home use. Use a propane "hot plate" with a platform big enough to heat your tank. When you run the wort into the brewkettle, bring it to a full, rolling boil so that it's almost jumping out of the surface of the pot. A low, simmering boil doesn't get rid of the sulfur compounds that come out of the malt and will leave too many off flavors in the finished beer.

Beer needs a lot of air in order to ferment. If you don't have enough oxygen in the wort to get the process started, it will just sit there. Aerate the wort prior to fermentation with pure oxygen, if you can buy it in a reasonably sized tank.

Good scales are essential. You also need, at least, a hydrometer or similar device that lets you measure the specific gravity of the wort and the specific gravity of the beer while it's fermenting.

Here are some helpful hints for home brewing some of the styles we make at Grant's:

Scottish Ale

Use a good, vigorous Scottish ale yeast, Cascade hops (for its distinctive character), and a lot of caramel malt or caramel malt syrup (I prefer the English syrup varieties). Employ fairly mild mashing conditions. Carefully control the fermentation temperatures, shooting for about 72 degrees Fahrenheit.

Imperial Stout

To make a good imperial or foreign-style stout, you should have original gravity of about 18 degrees Plato, so that you come out with 7 or 8 percent alcohol. Besides using black malt to give you the color (and I think a stout should be absolutely black), I would use a lot of caramel malt (probably 20 percent of the grist) to give you the body, along with the butterscotch character that is important in a good stout. Use lots of hops to get the bitterness units up to at least 50, preferably 70 to 75. Boil the hops a long time. To my mind, you don't want a lot of hop aroma in a good stout. You want that burnt barley, burnt malt aroma.

India Pale Ale

Use all malt. Brew it at a decent gravity—at least 12 degrees Plato—in order to produce a higher concentration of flavors and strength. You need mash for residual carbohydrates. Use lots of the right kind of hops, such as Galena for a nice, sharp, clean bitterness and not much aroma, which is what I look for in an IPA. A common mistake is using too much hops. It should be bitter, but not too bitter. I like my hops to show, but not to totally dominate all the flavor in the beer. It's a balancing act. At 50 bitterness units, a moderate-strength IPA like mine is just about right; 75 would be too much.

Hefeweizen

The Germans say to use at least 50 percent wheat malt, but you can get by with 25 to 35 percent. We use two different yeasts in our American version: a standard ale yeast for primary fermentation, then a more powdery yeast that we leave in the beer, so it's present in the bottles and kegs. You may want to use a traditional Bavarian hefeweizen yeast if you like their distinctive "banana and clove" aromas and flavors.

I recommend a moderate amount of hops. Many hefeweizens are way too bland—you see the cloudiness, but you don't get much taste. Very few of them have any hop flavor or aroma. In hefeweizen, hops should be minimal but still noticeable. At least 25 percent of the hops should be aroma varieties that are added at the end of the boil, so that you get a little more than just the yeast character. I shoot for about 20 BUs.

Porter

You have to brew porter by trial and error because you can go off balance quickly. You can write out a recipe, but you still have to balance it for your own taste. You won't get it right the first time around. You'll have to taste it to see if there's too much caramel malt or peat-smoked malt, or not enough oak chips (during maturation). A little bit more of the peat malt, and that's all you'd notice; too much caramel and not enough of the black malt, you'd get beer that's too sweet. The first one we did wasn't bad, but it was much too smoky, so we had to cut that way back. Then we balanced out on the caramel malt and came up with the right body.

Keep It Clean

Many beginning home brewers hate to dump anything. My advice is, if you made a mistake, admit it, and then dump the beer and start over. If you don't, you might get used to awful-flavored beer.

Then after you're done, immediately empty everything that has water or beer in it. Wash those items that will fit in a dishwasher or use unscented detergent and lots of hot water.

If you let a few days go by before cleaning your equipment, then you'll have to deal with crusty residue that's very hard to remove. But if you discipline yourself to scour everything clean right away, it comes off easily, clean as a whistle. Our brewery has more hot water rinses, hand washing and pot scrubbing than a hospital surgical ward.

If you clean things thoroughly—and I mean thoroughly—and let them dry, you don't need to sterilize with bleach. That's probably one of the worst things you can do, particularly when you're using plastic fermenters or tubing, because it's very difficult to get rid of the disinfectant flavor once it's locked in.

So once everything is clean and dry, then you can relax, and wait for your beer to ferment. Don't rush the process. Be patient. Then you can sit back and sip your beer.

Not too long ago, Grant's was the only brewery to receive a top award for every beer we entered in the international Cheers One World Beer Festival. Here's to a "heavy medal" future!

Chapter Twelve

WHERE DO WE GO FROM HERE?

Through the first 13 years of our brewery, I believe we led the craft brewing industry in terms of the quality and taste of our beer, but we weren't inspirational in terms of making money or rapid expansion or marketing. Still, we had lost money in only 2 of our 13 years, and we always had a continuing upward trend in sales.

By the end of 1995, as the competition continued to increase, it appeared that for us to stay in the game, it was going to take far more money than I could raise. It had gotten to the point where I was spending more time worrying about money than I was about beer. And that's not what I want to do with the rest of my life.

Unlike our rival microbreweries, I didn't want to have a public offering of stock, put out a prospectus and promise investors the moon. I wanted a situation in which I would be the owner or just the brewmaster, but with set rules. The most important of those is rule number one: beer quality first.

So, in November 1995, when Allen Shoup, president of International Wine & Spirits, offered me the opportunity to be permanent brewmaster and consultant, in exchange for selling his company the whole thing, I thought it was a great deal. The management company for I.W.S. is called Stimson Lane Vineyards & Estates. Stimson Lane runs acclaimed wineries like Chateau Ste. Michelle and Columbia Crest in Washington State, and Villa Mt. Eden in Napa Valley. They would provide the expertise we lacked in sales, marketing and distribution, and help expand our market.

What attracted me to the deal, when I was negotiating with Allen Shoup, was that we both agreed that *quality comes first*. His company's success was based on producing great wine, and ours was based on producing great beer. That was the number-one priority for both of us.

Stimson Lane invested in new, more and better equipment, a new pilot brewery, and a new identity and packaging for Bert Grant's Ales. That really is my mug on the label. If we needed to, we now could brew as much as 50,000 barrels per year on a 24-hour-a-day operation. Best of all, with Stimson Lane's increased distribution muscle, our beers now arrive on the market fresher and in better condition.

The change has allowed me to take a more active part in spreading the word about Grant's Ales. I remain in charge of quality control and new product development. No changes are made without my approval. This company will continue to march to a different drummer, and that drummer is me. If I don't like a beer, it doesn't get my name on it. I still work 15 hours a day. When word got out that I was contemplating selling the brewery, a lot of people thought I was going to retire. I told them that I was *not* retiring. This is my *life*. That's why I have a special arrangement with Stimson Lane: they can't fire me, and I can't quit!

BREWER CONFERENCES

I've always maintained my love of chemistry. I'm probably the only guy in the world who ever gave different professional research papers to the European Brewing Congress, the Master Brewers Association of the Americas, and the American Society of Brewing Chemists in the same year. I like giving papers based on my own research. That's the scientist in me.

THE STATE OF BREWING

With the rapid growth in the numbers of small breweries and brewpubs during the late 1980s and early 1990s, the American beer-drinking public has an unprecedented range of products to choose from. All of them together, though, represent only a microscopic 3 percent of the beer industry. Of course, when I started, the percentage was zero.

The country's six largest brewers still make more than 90 percent of the beer, and they are getting smarter. They each have expanded from an average of three or four leading house brands to about eight or nine. Many of these are "light," "dry" or "draft" versions of the standard American lager. Some, however, are showing real taste changes, with the latest trend being (surprise!) a return to "all malt" and a noticeable increase in hop flavor. A-B and Miller do a lot of microbrew look-alikes: they add food coloring or throw in a token amount of roast barley, and call it "Pink Dog" or something. A-B also has been buying into the biggest microbreweries, including Redhook and Widmer Brewing.

Then there are the contract brewers. These guys get my dander up! To me, they are just a bunch of promoters who are jumping on the bandwagon. They convince underutilized major breweries to brew "their grand-dad's special recipe," with all the economies of scale involved, and then turn around and sell it to consumers at a price comparable to that of a real craft brew. We make our beer and sell it for a 20 percent markup, theoretically. These guys can take anywhere up to a 150 percent markup. They may know how to make money, but I don't think they know much about beer.

But I think people are finally catching on. I would like to see the contract brewers replaced by the big breweries making good beer and promoting it under their own name. If A-B, Miller or Stroh is actually making the stuff, then *their* name should be on the label. The Michelob and Henry Weinhard's lines of specialty ales and lagers are a step in the right direction from this promotional standpoint; you can make up your own mind about the beer.

Looking in my crystal ball, I envision craft brewing continuing to grow to a point at which real craft beer will capture between 5 and 6 percent of the overall market. I can see having a brewpub for every 100,000 people in North America.

What It's All About

When it comes to beer, I have always wanted to do something different from the mainstream. As I said earlier, I think beer should reflect the taste of its brewer. I want to make the best beer I can with the best ingredients I can find, regardless of cost.

And whether it's about the name of Perfect Porter or the re-creation of India Pale Ale, I like to think the best beers have stories behind them. Here's one of my favorites:

Several years ago, we took cask-conditioned versions of our Imperial Stout and Scottish Ale to the Great British Beer Festival, which was held in a big hall in Brighton, England. It's this huge celebration of British brewing, almost a statement of national pride, given how much the Brits love their ale. We were one of only four American breweries represented at the "foreign beer bar."

This very large longshoreman-type walked up to our table. He was a scruffy-looking character—big, hairy and sweaty—with tattoos all over his arms. He looked up at our American flag and sneered. Looking like he was going to pound my head into the ground, he stared at the Imperial Stout tap handle and said, in his roughest English accent, "Stout, eh? I'll try it."

I poured him a glass. He picked it up, sniffed it and took a sip.

In an instant, his face transformed from a scowl to an absolutely beatific smile—I've never seen anyone's face change so fast. I'll never forget what he said next.

"Gorgeous!" he declared. "Absolutely bloody gorgeous!"

Best accolade I've ever been given.